AUTOBIOGRAPHY

I AM twenty-eight years old, and was born and attended school in Huntington, W. Va. My people were working people. My father started to work in a coal-mine when he was eight years old. Later, he became a glass blower, and unable to afford medical treatment, died of cancer at the age of forty-four. There were five children and I was the oldest. My mother took my father's place in the factory. My father's father was crushed to death in a coal-mine. My father never hoped for anything better in this life than a job, and never worried about anything else but losing it. My mother never wanted anything else than that the kids get an education so that they wouldn't have to worry about the factory closing down.

I worked in glass factories and proof-read on newspapers at nights while going through three years of college. I remember that the Art Appreciation book was pink, and the Biology book was green. Other than that, I do not remember very much about my college education. I taught for two years in mountain schools in West Virginia. I do not remember anything memorable about that except that Emil, one of my star pupils, who invariably made six on the Intelligence Tests, and who wanted to do nothing in school or in life but catch flies and pull their wings out, caught fifty-four flies in one day without ever having completely left the edge of his seat. At the end of nine months I had taught him to count to sixty, which, I felt, left a wide margin of safety in Emil's life for any emergency which might come up. Since the best that he had ever done under any other teacher was forty-three flies, and as far as I know he never beat fifty-four, I feel that I was a passing success as a school teacher.

At twenty-three I started out for Kansas to make the wheat harvest. My intentions were to hitch-hike, and after hiking all day without a lift, a freight train pulled to a stop beside the road. I crawled into a box car. I never again voluntarily took up the responsibilities of hitch-hiking, but I always aligned my interests with the interests of the railroad companies. They generally got me where I wanted to go, which was never more definite than "east" or "west."

There were no jobs in Kansas. The Combine had come, and I got my first taste of men trying to buck a machine. I got my first taste of going three days without food, and walking up to a back door and dinging a woman for a hand-out. It was a yellow house, but not too yellow, and I made it. Since then I have hit a thousand such yellow houses and have never been turned down. Women who live in green houses will not even open the door for me.

I remained on the fritz for five months and came home. There was no work at home. I bummed to California and then back again to New York and Washington, D. C. I was sentenced to sixty days in Occoquam Prison in Washington for sleeping in an empty building during a storm. Some friends got me out in eight days. I did not like Washington after that and came home and hunted for work for three months. There wasn't any work, and it was about that time that people started laughing at you for asking for work. After a while I stopped asking for work. I started out again and have been on the road almost constantly since then, except for fifteen months I spent in a C.C.C. camp. This last time has been four years. Sometimes I would stay in a town for four or five months doing odd jobs for a room and something to eat. Most of the time I slept and ate in missions, dinged the streets and houses, and used every other racket known to stiffs to get by.

I had no idea of getting *Waiting for Nothing* published, therefore, I wrote it just as I felt it, and used the language that stiffs use even when it wasn't always the nicest language in the world.

Parts of the book were scrawled on Bull Durham papers in box cars, margins of religious tracts in a hundred missions, jails, one prison, railroad sand-houses, flop-houses, and on a few memorable occasions actually pecked out with my two index fingers on an honest-to-God typewriter.

Save for four or five incidents, it is strictly autobiographical. Some of the events portrayed did not occur in the same sequence as I gave them, for I have juggled them in order to better develop the story. The "Stiff" idiom is, of course, authentic.

TOM KROMER

WAITING
FOR
NOTHING

TOM KROMER

 AMERICAN CENTURY SERIES
HILL AND WANG · NEW YORK

TO

JOLENE

WHO TURNED OFF THE GAS

Copyright 1935 by Alfred A. Knopf, Inc.
All rights reserved
Library of Congress catalog card number: 68-14793

ISBN (clothbound edition): 0-8090-9655-2
ISBN (paperback edition): 0-8090-0089-X

First American Century Series edition March 1968

Printed in the United States of America
234567890

WAITING
FOR
NOTHING

CHAPTER ONE

It is night. I am walking along this dark street, when my foot hits a stick. I reach down and pick it up. I finger it. It is a good stick, a heavy stick. One sock from it would lay a man out. It wouldn't kill him, but it would lay him out. I plan. Hit him where the crease is in his hat, hard, I tell myself, but not too hard. I do not want his head to hit the concrete. It might kill him. I do not want to kill him. I will catch him as he falls. I can frisk him in a minute. I will pull him over in the shadows and walk off. I will not run. I will walk.

I turn down a side street. This is a better street. There are fewer houses along this street. There are large trees on both sides of it. I crouch behind one of these. It is dark here. The shadows hide me. I wait. Five, ten minutes, I wait. Then under an arc light a block away a man comes walking. He is a well-dressed man. I can tell even from that distance. I have good eyes. This guy will be in the dough. He walks with his head up and a jaunty step. A stiff does not walk like that. A stiff shuffles with tired feet, his head huddled in his coat collar. This guy is in the dough. I can tell that. I clutch my stick tighter. I notice that I am calm. I am not scared. I am calm. In the crease of his hat, I tell myself. Not too hard. Just hard enough. On he comes. I slink farther back in the shadows. I press closer against this tree. I hear his footsteps thud on the concrete walk. I raise my arm high. I must swing hard. I poise myself. He crosses in front of me. Now is my chance. Bring it down hard, I tell myself, but not too hard. He is under my arm. He is right under my arm, but my stick does not come down. Something has happened to me. I am sick in the stomach. I have lost my nerve. Christ, I have lost my nerve. I am shaking all over. Sweat stands out on my forehead. I can feel the clamminess of it in the cold, damp night. This will not do. This will not do. I've got to get me something to eat. I am starved.

I stagger from the shadows and follow behind

this guy. He had a pretty good face. I could tell as
he passed beneath my arm. This guy ought to be
good for two bits. Maybe he will be good for four
bits. I quicken my steps. I will wait until he is
under an arc light before I give him my story. I do
not have long to wait. He stops under an arc light
and fumbles in his pocket for a cigarette. I catch
up with him.

"Pardon me, mister, but could you help a hungry
man get—"

"You goddam bums give me a pain in the neck.
Get the hell away from me before I call a cop."

He jerks his hand into his overcoat pocket. He
wants me to think he has a gun. He has not got a
gun. He is bluffing.

I hurry down the street. The bastard. The dirty
bastard. I could have laid him out cold with the
stick. I could have laid him out cold with the stick,
and he calls me a goddam bum. I had the stick over
his head, and I could not bring it down. I am yellow. I can see that I am yellow. If I am not yellow,
why am I shaking like a leaf? I am starved, too, and
I ought to starve. A guy without enough guts to get
himself a feed ought to starve.

I walk on up the street. I pass people, but I let
them pass. I do not ding them. I have lost my nerve.
I walk until I am on the main stem. Never have I
been so hungry. I have got to get me something to

WAITING FOR NOTHING

eat. I pass a restaurant. In the window is a roast chicken. It is brown and fat. It squats in a silver platter. The platter is filled with gravy. The gravy is thick and brown. It drips over the side, slow. I stand there and watch it drip. Underneath it the sign says: "All you can eat for fifty cents." I lick my lips. My mouth waters. I sure would like to sit down with that before me. I look inside. It is a classy joint. I can see waitresses in blue and white uniforms. They hurry back and forth. They carry heavy trays. The dishes stick over the edge of the trays. There are good meals still left in these trays. They will throw them in the garbage cans. In the center of the floor a water fountain bubbles. It is made of pink marble. The chairs are red leather, bordered in black. The counter is full of men eating. They are eating, and I am hungry. There are long rows of tables. The cloths on them are whiter than white. The glassware sparkles like diamonds on its whiteness. The knives and forks on the table are silver. I can tell that they are pure silver from where I am standing on the street. They shine so bright. I cannot go in there. It is too classy, and besides there are too many people. They will laugh at my seedy clothes, and my shoes without soles.

I stare in at this couple that eat by the window. I pull my coat collar up around my neck. A man will look hungrier with his coat collar up around

6

his neck. These people are in the dough. They are in evening clothes. This woman is sporting a satin dress. The blackness of it shimmers and glows in the light that comes from the chandelier that hangs from the dome. Her fingers are covered with diamonds. There are diamond bracelets on her wrists. She is beautiful. Never have I seen a more beautiful woman. Her lips are red. They are even redder against the whiteness of her teeth when she laughs. She laughs a lot.

I stare in at the window. Maybe they will know a hungry man when they see him. Maybe this guy will be willing to shell out a couple of nickels to a hungry stiff. It is chicken they are eating. A chicken like the one in the window. Brown and fat. They do not eat. They only nibble. They are nibbling at chicken, and they are not even hungry. I am starved. That chicken was meant for a hungry man. I watch them as they cut it into tiny bits. I watch their forks as they carry them to their mouths. The man is facing me. Twice he glances out of the window. I meet his eyes with mine. I wonder if he can tell the eyes of a hungry man. He has never been hungry himself. I can tell that. This one has always nibbled at chicken. I see him speak to the woman. She turns her head and looks at me through the window. I do not look at her. I look at the chicken on the plate. They can see that

I am a hungry man. I will stand here until they come out. When they come out, they will maybe slip me a four-bit piece.

A hand slaps down on my shoulder. It is a heavy hand. It spins me around in my tracks.

"What the hell are you doin' here?" It is a cop.

"Me? Nothing," I say. "Nothing, only watching a guy eat chicken. Can't a guy watch another guy eat chicken?"

"Wise guy," he says. "Well, I know what to do with wise guys."

He slaps me across the face with his hand, hard. I fall back against the building. His hands are on the holster by his side. What can I do? Take it is all I can do. He will plug me if I do anything.

"Put up your hands," he says.

I put up my hands.

"Where's your gat?" he says.

"I have no gat," I say. "I never had a gat in my life."

"That's what they all say," he says.

He pats my pockets. He don't find anything. There is a crowd around here now. Everybody wants to see what is going on. They watch him go through my pockets. They think I am a stick-up guy. A hungry stiff stands and watches a guy eat chicken, and they think he is a stick-up guy. That is a hell of a note.

"All right," he says, "get down the street before I run you in. If I ever catch you stemming this beat, I will sap the living hell out of you. Beat it."

I hurry down the street. I know better than not to hurry. The lousy son of a bitch. I had a feed right in my lap, and he makes me beat it. That guy was all right in there. He was a good guy. That guy could see I was a hungry man. He would have fixed me up right when he came out.

I pass a small café. There are no customers in here. There is only a guy sitting by the cash register. This is my place. I go in and walk up to him. He is a fat guy with a double chin. I can see very well that he hasn't missed many meals in his life.

"Mister," I say, "have you got some kind of work like washing dishes I can do for something to eat? I am damn near starved. I'll do anything."

He looks hard at me. I can see right away that this guy is no good.

"Tell me," he says, "in God's name, why do you stiffs always come in here? You're the fourth guy in the last half-hour. I can't even pay my rent. There ain't been a customer in here for an hour. Go to some of the big joints where they do all the business."

"Could you maybe give me a cup of coffee?" I say. "That would hold me over. I've been turned down at about twenty places already."

WAITING FOR NOTHING

"I can't give you nothing. Coffee costs money," he says. "Go to one of the chain stores and bum your coffee. When you've got any money, where do you go to spend it? You go to the chains. I can't do nothing for you."

I walk out. Wouldn't even give a hungry man a cup of coffee. Can you imagine a guy like that? The bastard. I'd like to catch him on a dark street. I'd give him a cup of coffee, and a sock on the snout he wouldn't soon forget. I walk. When I pass a place where there are no customers, I go in. They turn me down flat. No business, they say. Why don't I go to the big places? I am getting sick in the stomach. I feel like vomiting. I have to get me something to eat. What the hell? I will hit me one of these classy joints. Pride! What do I care about pride? Who cares about me? Nobody. The bastards don't care if I live or die.

I pass a joint. A ritzy place. It is all white inside. The tables are full. The counters are full. They are eating, and I am hungry. These guys pay good dough for a feed, and they are not even hungry. When they are through, they will maybe tip the waitress four bits. It is going to be cold tonight. Four bits will buy me a flop that will be warm, and not cold.

I go into this joint and walk up to the middle of the counter. I flop down in a seat. These cash customers gape at me. I am clean, but my front is seedy. They know I don't belong in here. I know I don't belong in here, too. But I am hungry. A hungry man belongs where there is food. Let them gape.

This waiter sticks the menu out to me. I do not take it. What do I want with a menu?

"Buddy," I say, "I am broke and hungry. Could you maybe give me something to eat?"

He shakes his head no, he cannot give me anything to eat.

"Busy. Manager's not in. Sorry."

I can feel my face getting red. They are all gaping at me. They crane their necks to gape at me. I get up out of this seat and walk towards the door. I can't get anything to eat anywhere. God damn them, if I could get my fingers on a gat.

"Say, buddy."

I turn around. A guy in a gray suit is motioning to me. He sits at the middle of the counter. I go back.

"You hungry?"

"I'm damn near starved. I have not eat in two days, and that is the God's truth."

"Down on your luck?" he says.

"Down so far I don't know how far," I say.

"Sit down. I've been down on my luck myself. I know how it is."

I sit down beside him.

"What'll it be?" he says.

"You order it," I say. "Anything you say."

"Order up anything you want. Fill up."

"A ham sandwich and a cup of coffee," I tell this waiter.

He is all smiles now, damn him. He sees where he can make a dime. I bet he owns this joint. He said the manager wasn't in, and I bet he's the manager himself.

"Give him a beef-steak dinner with everything that goes with it," says this guy in the gray suit. "This man is hungry."

This is a good guy. He orders my steak dinner in a loud voice so everyone can see how big-hearted he is, but he is a good guy anyway. Any guy is a good guy when he is going to buy me a steak dinner. Let him show off a little bit. He deserves to show off a little bit. I sit here at this counter, and I feel like pinching myself. This is a funny world. Five minutes ago I was down in the dumps. Here I am now waiting on a steak dinner in a classy joint. Let them gape. What do I care? Didn't they ever see a hungry man before?

This waiter shoves my dinner in front of me. Christ, I've never seen anything look so good. This steak with all the trimmings is a picture for sore eyes. Big and thick and brown, it sits there. Around it, all around it, are tomatoes, sliced. I start in. I do not look up from my plate. They are all gaping at me. Fill up and get out of here, I tell myself.

The guy three seats down gets up and calls for his check. He is a little guy with horn-rimmed glasses. The check is thirty cents.I see it before the waiter turns it upside down. Why do they always have to turn a man's check upside down? Afraid the price will turn his stomach? This guy pulls a dollar out of his pocket and walks over to the cashier. I wonder how it feels to have a buck in your jeans. Four bits will set me on top of the world right now. A good warm flop tonight and breakfast in the morning. That's the way to live. Pay for what you get, and look every copper you pass on the street straight in the eye, and say: "You bastard, I don't owe you a cent."

The cashier hands this guy his change. He walks back and lays it down by my plate.

"Flop for tonight," he says.

He speaks low. He is not trying to show off like this guy in the gray suit. Not that I don't think that this guy in the gray suit is not all right. He is a good guy. He bought me a steak dinner when I was damn near starved. No, he is a good guy, but he likes to show off a little bit. I look up at this guy. He is walking out of the door. I do not thank him. He is too far away, and besides, what can I say?

I can't believe it. Thirty cents, the check said. Thirty cents from a dollar. That makes seventy cents. I got seventy cents. A good warm flop tonight, breakfast in the morning, and enough left over for cigarettes. No fishing around in the gutters for snipes for me. I will have me a package of tailor-made cigarettes. I pick up this change and stick it in my pocket. That guy is a mind-reader. I was sitting here wishing I had four bits, and before I know it, I got seventy cents. That guy is all right. I bet that guy has had troubles of his own some time. I bet he knows how it is to be hungry. I hurry up with my dinner. In here I am only a hungry stiff. Outside with seventy cents in my kick, I am as good as the next one. Say, I'd like to meet that guy, and I had a million dollars.

"Do you remember the time you give me seventy cents in a restaurant? You don't? Well, you give me seventy cents in a restaurant one time. I was damn near starved. I was just about ready to bump myself off, and you give me seventy cents."

I hand him a roll of bills. It is a big roll of bills. I walk off. That guy won't have to worry any more about dough. There was plenty in that roll to keep him in wheatcakes the rest of his life.

I finish my pie and get up.

"Thank you, Jack," I say to this guy in the gray suit. "I certainly appreciate what you done for me.

I was damn near starved."

"That's all right, buddy," he says. "Glad to help a hungry man."

He speaks loud. They can hear him to the other end of the counter. He is a good guy, though. He bought me a steak dinner.

I walk outside. I put my hand in my pocket and jingle my money. It feels good to have money to jingle. I am not broke or hungry now. I cannot imagine I was broke and hungry an hour ago. No park for me tonight. No lousy mission flop.

I go down the street and walk through the park. I look at these benches with their iron legs and their wooden slats.

"To hell with you," I say. "I have nothing to do with you. I do not know you. You will leave no grooves in my back tonight. Tonight I will have me a good warm flop. I will have me a flop that will be warm, and not cold."

I look at these stiffs sprawled out on the benches. I like to walk to the time of the jingle in my pocket and think how miserable I was last night.

It is getting late, and I am tired. I head down the skid road and stop in front of my four-bit flop. There is no marquee in front to keep the guests from getting wet. There is no doorman dressed like a major in the Imperial Guards. They do not need these things, because all the suites are on the

15

fourth floor. I am puffing when I get to the top of the rickety stairs. At the landing a guy squats on a stool in a wire cage.

"I want a four-bit flop," I say, "a four-bit flop with a clean bed."

This guy is hunched over a desk with his belly sticking out of a dirty green sweater. He rubs his hands together and shows his yellow teeth in a grin. He winks one of his puffy eyes.

"For a little extra, just a little extra," he says, "I can give you a nice room, a very nice room. But it is too big a room for one. You will be lonely. A little company will not go bad, eh? Especially if the company is very young and very pretty?" He licks his puffy lips. "We have a girl, a new girl. Only tonight she came. Because it is you, and she must learn, only a dollar extra, yes?"

I look at him, and I think of the fish-eyed, pot-bellied frogs I used to gig when I was a kid. I imagine myself sticking a sharp gig into his belly and watching him kick and croak.

"A four-bit flop is what I want," I say. "I do not wish to play nursemaid to your virgins. I am broke, and besides, I am sleepy."

"But you should see her," he says, "so tiny, so beautiful. I will get her. You will change your mind when you see her."

"I do not want to see her," I say.

"So high," he says. "Only so high she is, and so beautiful. I will get her. You will see how beautiful she is."

He climbs off his stool.

"Do I get me a flop or do I have to bury my foot in your dirty belly?" I say.

"Some other time, then," he says, "some other time when you have more money. You will see how very beautiful."

He waddles through the dirty hall. I follow him. His legs are swollen with dropsy. His ankles overflow his ragged house-slippers and hang down in folds over the sides. I can imagine I hear the water gurgling as he walks. He opens the door and holds out his hand for the money.

"How many beds in this room?" I say.

"Forty," he says, "but they are good, clean beds."

I walk into this room. It is a big room. It is filled with these beds. They do not look so hot to me. They are only cots. They look lousy. I bet they are lousy, but a stiff has got to sleep, lousy or not. Most of these beds are already full. I can hear the snores of the stiffs as they sleep. I pick me out a flop at the other end of the room. There is no mattress. Only two dirty blankets. They are smelly. Plenty of stiffs have slept under these blankets.

Four or five stiffs are gathered in a bunch over next to the wall. I watch them. I know very well

17

what they are going to do. They are gas hounds, and they are going to get soused on derail.

"Give me that handkerchief," says this red-headed guy with the wens on his face. "I will squeeze more alky out of a can of heat than any stiff I know."

This little guy with the dirty winged collar examines this can of heat.

"The bastards," he says. "You know what? They're makin' the cans smaller and smaller. This can right here is smaller than they was yestiddy. The dirty crooks. They'd take the bread right out of your mouths, the bastards would."

He jumps up and down as he talks. His red eyes flash. The sweat stands in beads on his forehead. How can a guy get so mad about the size of a can of heat? Well, it does not take much to make you mad when you have been swigging heat for a year.

This red-headed guy takes this can of heat and empties it out in a handkerchief. The handkerchief is filthy, but that don't worry them none. What's a little filth to a gas hound? Pretty soon they will be high and nothing will worry them. Pretty soon they won't have any more troubles. This derail will see to that. They squeeze this stuff out of the hand-kerchief and let it drip into the glass. They pour water into the glass. The smell of this stuff will turn your stomach, but it don't turn their stomach.

They are going to drink it. They take turns about taking a swig. They elbow each other out of the way to get at the glass. When it is all gone, they squeeze out some more. They choke and gag when this stuff goes down, but they drink it. Pretty soon they have guzzled all the heat they have. In a little while they are singing. I do not blame these guys for getting soused on derail. A guy can't always be thinking. If a guy is thinking all the time, pretty soon he will go crazy. A man is bound to land up in the booby-hatch if he stays on the fritz. So these guys make derail and drink it.

This stiff in the bed next to mine turns up his nose at these guys who are soused up on derail.

"I got my opinion of a guy who will drink derail," he says. "A guy who will drink derail is lower down than a skunk."

He pulls a bottle out from under his pillow. It is marked: "Bay Rum." There are directions on the label. It says it will grow new hair. It says it will stop the old from falling out. But this guy does not need this stuff to keep his hair from falling out. This stiff has not had a haircut for a year.

"This is the stuff," he says. "I have been drinkin' this old stuff for a year, and I don't even get a headache afterwards."

He sticks this bottle up to his trap, and he does not take it down until he has emptied it.

"This is good stuff," he says. "It has got derail beat all to a frazzle."

I do not see how it can be such good stuff when he has to gag so much when he downs it. But that is his business. If a guy has been drinking this stuff for a year, he ought to know if it is good stuff or not. Pretty soon this guy is dead to the world. He sprawls out on his bunk and sleeps. He sleeps with his eyes wide open. Christ, he gives me the willies with his eyes wide open like that. He looks like a dead man, but I never see a dead man with his face covered with sweat like his is. It is plenty chilly in this room, but his face is covered with sweat. That is the bay rum coming out of him. A guy that has been drinking this stuff for a year must have plenty inside him. I bet the inside of his gut is covered with hair. That would be a good way to find out if this bay rum is a fake or not. When this stiff croaks from swigging too much bay rum, just cut him open. If his gut is not covered with hair, then this bay rum is a fake.

I watch him. I cannot keep my eyes off him. His legs twitch. He quivers and jerks. He is having a spasm. He almost jumps off the bed. All the time his eyes are wide open, and the sweat pours out of him. But he does not know what it is all about. He is dead to the world. If this is the good stuff, I will take the bad stuff. I will not even put this stuff on my hair. I would be afraid it would sink down into my gut and give me the spasms like this guy has got. The rest of these stiffs do not pay any attention to him. These bay horse fiends are old stuff to them. But they are not old stuff to me. It gets on my nerves. If this guy is going to act like this all night, I am going to walk the streets. It will be cold as hell walking the streets all night, but it will not be as bad as watching this guy jump up and down with his eyes wide open, and him dead to the world.

I cover up my head with this dirty blanket and try not to think about him.

CHAPTER TWO

IT RAINS. It will rain all night, but I cannot stand here in the wet all night. I shiver in this doorway and watch this peroxide blonde in the red hat hurrying down the street. She jumps from awning to awning, and eyes the cars that plow through the water in the street. She is on the make, and soaked to the skin. The wind drives against her and through her and plasters her dress to her legs. She ducks into this doorway I am in.

"Think it'll rain, sweetheart?" she says.

"If it don't rain tonight, it will tomorrow," I say. "You can't never tell about rain."

"Got another cigarette, deary?" she says. "I'm dyin' for a cigarette."

I give her a cigarette. She pulls out a vanity case and looks at her face.

"Holy God," she says, "look at me. How's a girl goin' to keep her complexion in weather like this?"

"What are you kicking about?" I say. "You're alive, ain't you? It ain't wet. It only looks wet. The sun'll be up tomorrow, beautiful like."

She takes a swipe at her face with her handkerchief. It leaves a streak from her eyes to her chin. The water runs down the streak and drips off her chin in pink drops. She pulls her red hat off her head. It leaves a red smudge across her forehead.

"Tra, la la," she says. "How sweet the blue birdies sing! You flopped in a mission last night. I can tell by the way you talk you flopped in a mission. Look at this goddam hat. Just look at it. Limp as a rag. The goddam kike said it wouldn't fade. Now look at it. I oughta take it back and stuff it down his throat."

She wads it up in her hand and squeezes the water out of it. It makes a red pool at her feet.

"I see you once or twice in Grumpy's hashhouse," I say. "I eat in Grumpy's when I'm lucky on the stem."

"Pleased to meet you socially," she says. "Call me Myrtle. I only eat in Grumpy's for the change. Most of the time I am up on the Avenoo with the swells."

"My name is Tom," I say. "I am expecting a registered letter, myself."

She wipes her face off with her handkerchief and puts on a new coat of paint.

"My hair ain't naturally blond," she says; "I dyed it."

"Yeah?" I say. "You'd never know it."

"Yeah," she says, "I dyed it, and the goddam stuff cost me my job. 'Six blondes is enough for one house,' the madam says. 'Dye 'er black or get out.' 'Like hell I'll dye 'er black,' I says. 'Me spend five bucks for a dye, and then spend five more to ruin it? Not on your fanny,' I says."

"Fire you?"

"Right out on the street. Throws my clothes out on the street and pushes me out on top of them, the old whore."

"How is the street?" I say. "Tough?"

"Tough?" she says. "Say, I ain't seen a live one all day. I jumped in and out of so many doorways I got the jitters."

She peels her eyes across the street. There is a guy standing over there in a doorway. He is a young guy with a sporty front. There are gray spats on his kicks, and white kid gloves on his hands.

"Do you see what I see?" she says.

"Has he give you a tumble?" I say.

"Watch me land him," she says. "This is the first

live one I seen all day. I'll let you ding him before I reel him in."

"Thanks," I say. "I could use a few nickels till my registered letter gets in."

"Watch my technic," she says.

I keep my eyes peeled on this guy across the street. He is falling for the bait, all right. He shifts his eyes from her to me. He does not know what to think of me. He makes up his mind. He crosses the street and stops beneath this awning. He whistles low under his breath and keeps time with the drum of his fingers on the window. This is my chance to make a flop.

"Buddy," I say, "could you spare me a few dimes to get a flop? I'm down on my luck with no place to flop."

He looks at me and smiles. I can see that this guy is all right.

"Buddy," he says, "do you know what I would do if I was down on my luck with no place to get in out of the rain?"

"No, what would you do?" I say.

"I would get me a job and go to work," he says.

He turns his back on me and walks over to the girl.

"Hello, good-looking," he says.

"Hello, yourself," she says.

The lousy bastard. And I thought this guy was

all right. Go to work, would he? Does he think I would be standing here in the rain and the cold if there was work to be had? There is no work. They laugh at you for asking for work. I give this smart guy a look and walk on down the street. When I hit the skid road, I stop under another awning. I can see that I am not the only one in the wet and the cold. Old Bacon Butts hobbles up the street and stops by my side. I met him in the mission. When he is not gassed up on bay rum, he talks of blowing up the banks.

"Well, well, my little spewm of the system," he says, "where do you flop tonight?"

"On the street," I say. "I am not holding a jitney."

"Say not so," he cackles. His bloodshot eyes sparkle. He is gassed up plenty. "For the meek in spirit, the International House."

We walk through the rain, Bacon Butts and me. It beats down on his matted hair and drizzles through his beard. The drops sparkle like diamonds as the street-lights flash on his face. I almost have to grin when I think of diamonds in old Bacon Butts's beard. He would pick them out and swap them for bay rum.

We walk.

"Rain all you damn please," I think. "You can't hurt me. I'm as wet as I can get. I'm soaked to the skin. You can't hurt me."

"I'm an old man," whines old Bacon Butts, "an old, old, man, and I gotta go huntin' me a rat-hole at night."

"Yeah, it's hell," I say.

I can't be shedding any tears over old Bacon Butts. I have to find me a rat-hole myself. Besides, he is gassed up.

"I worked hard in my day," he says. "Worked like a horse and broke my health, and now I ain't got a decent place to flop."

His old voice cracks. His puffy eyes fill with tears.

"Yeah," I say, "that's tough. That sure is tough, that is. There ain't no justice in this world. A man just don't get a square deal in this world."

Old Bacon Butts takes another swig from his bottle. He sobs short, cackly sobs in his coat collar.

We turn left down this alley. Half-way down we slip through the doorway of this empty building. We tiptoe upstairs and go into this room. There are other stiffs in this room. We can hear them snore. We strike matches to keep from stepping on them. In one corner is a pile of burlap sacks. They are dry. Good enough for a couple of drowned rats hunting a hole.

I spread my bed upon the floor. I pull off my wet clothes and crawl naked between the sacks. Christ, but it feels good to be lying here. It is cold outside. I can hear the patter of the rain beating down on the tin roof. It is wet outside and cold. But I am not wet or cold. I am warm and dry.

"To hell with you," I say. "Rain all you damn please. I am warm."

It is good to be warm and dry. I had a good beef stew today. My belly is full. What have I got to worry about? Nothing. Nothing to worry about until tomorrow. I pull these sacks up around my chin and I think about those poor bastards out in the rain. They are wet and cold. But I am warm and dry. My eyes get heavy. I fall asleep.

I do not know how long I am asleep. I awake with a jerk. All around me are lights. They flash back and forth. It seems as though there are a thousand lights that flash through the dark. I hear a rat squeal and scurry across the floor. What the hell? I am half asleep, but I know that there is something wrong. My heart pounds. It chokes me. I am afraid. I hear heavy shoes thudding on the floor. I hear stiffs running back and forth and yelling at the top of their voices. A light flashes into my eyes and blinds me.

"Get up out of there," says a voice. "Get up out of there before I kick the living hell out of you."

I know what it is now. It is the bulls. Jesus Christ, can't they ever let a man alone? A man can't even sleep. You can't crawl into an empty rat-hole, for the bulls. This bull grabs me by the throat and yanks me to my feet. I reach over and bundle my clothes up in my arms. He thinks maybe I am reaching for a gat or a club. I feel his fist smash into my mouth. I feel the blood that oozes from my lips. I dress as they shove us outside. There are a bunch of cops out here. There are a bunch of stiffs herded between them. They are red-eyed and sleepy.

"Your paws tough?" this cop says to me.

"They oughta be," I say. "I done enough hard work in my day."

"Well, they better be," he says. "It's the rock pile for you lousy bums."

"Where's the rock pile?" says one of these stiffs.

"They're diggin' a ditch four miles long, and they need some help," this copper says.

"You lousy stiffs will have a place to flop tomorrow night," chirps in this other one.

I want to take this bull by his dirty neck and choke him till his tongue hangs out. The bastard has got himself a place to flop; what does he care about us? I don't say anything, though. They would sap me down proper if I said anything. I am on to their little tricks. I huddle down as far as I can go in my coat collar, but it does no good. The rain beats down in sheets. It drizzles through my clothes. Here I am soggy and miserable. There it was warm and dry.

Down the street shrieks a siren. It is the black Maria come to get us. She pulls up at the curb. They open the door.

"Taxi?" says this stiff with the wooden leg. "I didn't call any taxi."

"All right, haul in, and make it snappy," says this cop.

We get in. I am lucky. I get a seat. They crowd all of us in here like cattle. We are cattle to them. Damn them. Some day they will pay for this. For ten minutes we gasp in here. We are packed like sardines.

"Blow 'em up," yelps old Bacon Butts. He is down on the floor with two stiffs using him for a stool. "Blow the bastards up. Ram a stick of dynamite up their fannies. One stick for every copper. Give me a good dark box car. Give me a good sharp knife, and a copper to use it on. 'So, you bastard, you will throw me into a lousy patrol wagon, will you? Take that and that.' Give me a dark box car and a good sharp knife, and I will pull their yellow guts out with my bare hands."

A stiff crams his hat into old Bacon Butts's mouth. It will not do for the coppers to hear a stiff talking like this. It doesn't matter to a copper if he is gassed up or not.

We pull to a stop. We pile out in front of the precinct jail and hurry inside to get out of the rain. More bulls meet us at the door and start frisking us.

"Got a gat?" this cop snaps at the guy with the scarred face.

"What the hell would I be doin' with a gat? I am out of work and cain't find any work," he says.

"You're a goddam liar. You're a lousy bum, and you wouldn't work if you had work."

"Yeah," this stiff says, "that's what you think."

"Open your trap to me again, and I will kick the living hell out of you. Next."

I am next. I walk up in front of this cop. I hold out my arms from my sides. I know how to do it. I have been frisked more times than I got fingers and toes.

"An old-timer, eh?" he says. "How many times you been here before?"

"None," I say.

"Got a gat?"

"No, sir."

The dumb bastard. If I am holding a gat, does he think I will tell him? He goes through my pockets.

"Got a razor?"

"I got a safety razor."

"That's a razor, ain't it. I asked you did you have

31

a razor. I didn't ask you for any of your lip."

"Yes, sir," I say. The bastard.

"Got any money?"

"I got a ten-cent piece."

"You dirty bums never have any money. You never will have any money. You are no damn good, the whole bunch of you. Next."

I go over to the guy at the desk.

"What name did you give the last time?" he says.

"No name," I say. "There wasn't any last time."

"All right, Jesse James, what's the handle this time?"

"Thomas Kromer," I say.

Does this smart bastard think I will make up a name? What do I care who knows I am in this lousy can? The tight sons of bitches wouldn't give me a drink of water if my tongue was hanging out.

"My home is in Huntington, West Virginia," I say. I know all of these questions. I want to get it over with. I am sleepy. A guy can't even get a chance to sleep.

"Who in the hell asked you where your home was?" he says. "Your home is wherever you can find some rotten swill to stuff in your bellies."

"Sorry," I say.

"Occupation?" he says. "Anything that pops in your head. Song-writer, sky pilot, anything."

"Mechanic," I say.

"Age?"

"Twenty-six." Will this bastard never be finished with his questions?

"You'll be six months older when you get out. Next."

A cop shoves me into a big room. It is lined on all sides with cells. It will turn your stomach with the stench of unflushed commodes. The turnkey unlocks the door of one of these holes and shoves me in. He locks it and goes back after another stiff. I look around. There are two bunks on the wall. One on top of the other. A drunk is sprawled out in each of them. They have vomited all over the floor. I wonder where in the hell do they expect a guy to sleep. It is two o'clock in the morning. Do they think I am going to stand on my feet all night? If they do, they are crazy. The bastards. What do they care if I have to stand on my feet all night? I hammer on this steel door with my hands. I have to pound a long time before anybody comes to the door.

"What do you want in there?" It is the turnkey.

"Where is a guy going to sleep in here? There's drunks in both bunks, and the floor looks like a privy."

"Sleep on your head, Lily-fingers," he says, "or

33

on your pink teddies."

"I ain't slept in two nights, and I gotta get me some sleep," I say.

"What the hell do I care where you sleep?" he says. "You pound on that door again, and I will come in there and sap you down." He goes away.

A young punk with fuzz on his face sticks his nose through the bars of the cell across the hall.

"What you in for?" he says.

"Vag," I say. "I slept in an empty building to get in out of the rain, and they send me up for vag."

"Vag!" he says. "Hell, you ain't growed up yet. You know what I'm in here for?"

"No, what are you in here for?" I say.

"A hold-up, that's what I'm in here for," he says, "a hold-up."

This is a smart punk. He is not dry behind the ears yet. He is stuck on himself because he got caught pulling a stick-up. I let him gas through the bars. I do not pay any attention to him.

This guy in the next cell sticks his nose out.

"Like your suite, deary?" he yells.

He has a squeaky voice. I can see that his eyebrows are plucked, from where I am. This guy is as queer as they make them.

"Yeah, I like it fine," I say.

"The bitches," he says. "The goddam bitches.

34

WAITING FOR NOTHING

They raided my flat and broke up my date. A girl can't even have a decent date without the goddam cops breaking in."

This guy lying on the bunk gets up and shoves this queer away from the bars. He is a wolf. He does not want this pansy to be talking to me. He is jealous.

"For Christ sake, Florence, set down so's I can get me some sleep," he says.

I walk up and down the floor. Up and down. I keep this up for hours. I can't stand it any longer. I sit down in a corner and put my head in my hands. I am all in. Before I know it, I am dead to the world. I do not awake until morning.

"Water," moans the drunk in the top bunk, "for God's sake, won't someone give me some water?"

Nobody pays any attention to him. The drunk in the bottom bunk gets to his feet. I start to crawl in his bunk. I've got to get me some sleep. He clenches up his fists and starts towards me. I could kill him, but I get back in my corner. No use to have any trouble with a drunk.

"You're a bastard," he says. "Ain'tcha a bastard? You're a lousy bum. You're all lousy bums. The bastards won't keep me in here. I got dough. I'll show 'em, the bastards won't keep me in here. Take my money away from me, will they?" He leans over to me. "I'm too smart for these cops. I

35

put most of my money in my shoe."

He takes off his shoe and reaches down in the toe. He pulls out a wad of bills.

"So they think they can outsmart me, do they? I'm drunk, but I ain't nobody's fool."

He waves this dough around in the air. I see one of the bills drop to the floor. I put my foot on it. I figure it is mine by rights of my having my foot on it. He crawls back in his bunk and goes to sleep. I put this fin down in the toe of my shoe and sit back in my corner.

I wait for breakfast. That is a good joke. For two hours I squat in this corner before the turnkey opens the door.

"Where's my breakfast?" I say.

"Breakfast, hell!" he says. "There ain't no breakfast. It's the court for you bums."

They load us in the black Maria and take us to court. We pull in at the back door. They hand us a ham sandwich. We eat it and march to the courtroom and the prisoner's box. There are thirty of us stiffs here. There will have to be two trials. The prisoner's box is not big enough to hold us all. You won't read a better joke than this in a book. Don't they know a stiff has got to sleep?

A guy with a bald head and a black bow tie starts reading a paper. He is telling us what we are charged with. He mumbles something about no visible means of support. He mumbles something about vagrancy. What this guy means is, we slept in an empty building to get in out of the rain. He don't say that, though. He says we have no visible means of support. Does he think I would sleep in that lousy building if I was holding anything? We don't understand all this guy mumbles. We don't listen very close. We are too sleepy. He stops reading. The judge looks up. He has a hard face. Well, hard face or not, what can he do to a guy for sleeping? A guy has got to sleep.

"What have you got to say for yourself?" this judge asks the first guy.

"I am out of work. Last night it was rainin', and I didn't have any place to sleep. I—"

"Next."

"I have been sick. I was afraid of gettin' wet, so I—"

"Next."

"I am out of work and—"

"Next."

These guys don't get a chance to say anything. They no more than get started than he goes to the next guy. He is kangarooing them. They haven't got a chance. I am down near the end of the box. I make up my mind to make a hit. I have a good education. Let me see. I will plead guilty with mitigating circumstances. That sounds all right.

This judge will see that I am no ordinary stiff.

"Your honor," I will say very polite, "I am guilty, with mitigating circumstances."

The rest of these stiffs will perk up their ears when they hear this. They will not know what mitigating circumstances are, but the judge will know.

"Explain the mitigating circumstances," he will say.

"Your honor, as you know very well, the nation is faced with a world-wide crisis in unemployment. There are three things which are prime requisites of every civilized man, and even savage. These things are food, clothing, and shelter. We are confronted with the necessity of crime or beggary. It is inevitable, your honor, one choice or the other must be made. Rather than degrade ourselves with stealing, we are compelled to beg for the mite we eat. But we must sleep. Somewhere, your honor, we must sleep. In good weather we sleep in the parks. But yesterday it rained. The parks were soaked. This building was empty. We did not break in. It was empty. We had no alternative. We must sleep. We cannot sleep in the rain."

This will give this judge a rough idea. The trouble with these stiffs is they haven't got the guts to speak up. They are scared to death of this judge. Hell, this judge is no better than any other stiff to me. I will stand up for my rights. I will plead guilty with mitigating circumstances. I bet his ears will perk up when he hears a stiff pleading guilty with mitigating circumstances.

He comes on down the line. I go over my spiel in my head. I will be polite, but I will show this guy I am just as good as the next one. He gets to me.

"What have you got to say for yourself?" he says.

"Your honor," I say, "I am guilty with—"

"That's all I want to know. Next."

He don't give me a chance to say anything. I will not stand for this. I don't have to stand for this. Can you imagine a guy like this? They call this a free country, and this guy don't give me a chance to say anything. Maybe they can pull this on some of these stiffs with no education, but they can't pull it on me. I have got a good education. I've had good jobs in my time. I had privileges then, and I got privileges now. I stand up on my feet. Everybody looks at me. This judge gets red in the face. He yells for me to sit down. I do not sit down. All the coppers yell for me to sit down. Everybody is craning their necks to see what is going on. A big, fat woman with a red dress and a pocked face stands up in her seat and thrashes her hands in the air.

"Sock the old judge on the beezer," she yells at me. "Take a poke at the cossacks."

A cop plops her down in her seat. Another cop

pulls out a blackjack and starts over to me. What the hell can I do against a cop with a blackjack? He would sap me down proper, and all the rest of these cops would help him. A stiff hasn't got a chance. They know a stiff hasn't got a chance. I sit down.

This judge stands up. He is burned up, and his face is flaming red.

"Sixty days, or a hundred dollars. Take them away."

CHAPTER THREE

I sit down at the table in this mission. They shove this stew before us. It is awful. It smells bad. The room is full of the stench of this rotten stew. What am I going to do? What can I do? I am a hungry man. Food is food to a hungry man, whether it is rotten or not. I've got to eat. I take up a spoonful of this stuff and gag. As hungry as I am, I can't down this swill. This slop is not fit for hogs. I push it away and pick up the bread. This bread is hard and stale, but it hits the spot. Who am I to say it is no good? I've got to eat. This stiff next to me at the table leans far over his plate and goes after his swill. He is hungrier than I am.

"Ain'tcha goin' ter eat yer stew?" he says to me.

41

"No, I can't go this stuff."

"Kin I have it?"

"Take it, and welcome," I say.

He reaches over and takes my stew. He ladles up a spoonful. He makes a slushing noise when he sucks it in. I don't pay any attention. If a guy wants to suck in his swill, who am I to get my stomach turned? I have seen the day when I would have socked a guy on the kisser who sat next to me and made a noise like that. But that was before I went on the fritz. I used to wear spats then. Imagine me wearing spats now. I can stand on a dime and tell you whether it is heads or tails. That's how thin the soles of my kicks are.

This guy socks in another spoonful. He gulps and chokes. He sticks his fingers down his throat and pulls out a yellow overcoat button. What are these bastards putting yellow overcoat buttons in the stew for? Have they run out of their rotten carrots? Don't they know you can't make a decent stew out of yellow overcoat buttons? This stiff holds this yellow overcoat button up in the air.

"Looky," he yells down the table, "looky what I found. Any you blokes need a button fer yer overcoat?"

"See can you find a gray overcoat button," this stiff at the other end of the table yells. "My overcoat is gray. I can't be puttin' yellow overcoat buttons on a gray coat."

"Today is yellow overcoat button day. You kin not be gittin' yer choice of buttons till comes hash day," this stiff says. "A stiff kin not be gittin' his choice of buttons ever' day."

Another guy digs down in his stew.

"Wait till I see can I find needle and thread. You gotta have needle and thread."

These other stiffs start digging down in their stew to see can they find needle and thread. Not all of them, though. Four or five guys gag and get up from the table. These are hungry men, but the yellow overcoat button turns their stomach. They will soon get over that. I was like that once. That was when I used to wear spats.

This mission stiff who is the overseer of the kitchen walks up the aisle.

"What's eatin' you stiffs?" he yells. "Any more racket out of you, and I will throw you out in the street."

"Cain't a stiff do a little huntin'?" this old guy with all the badges pinned on him says.

"What the hell are you huntin' for?" he says.

"I am huntin' fer me a watch and chain," says one of these stiffs. "How kin I tell what time you feed, if I don't have me a watch and chain?"

"That is good stew," says this mission stiff. "I watched them make that stew myself."

"She ain't sech good stew," says this old man with the badges. "I cain't find me a overcoat. She is purty frosty out. I sure would like to find me a overcoat." He digs down in his stew.

These other stiffs all start to laugh. This mission stiff is getting his dander up.

"What the hell are you talkin' about?" he says. "Get out of here before I call a cop."

This old guy grins and beats it outside. He does not mind missing his supper. You will find better suppers than this in the sewers.

I sip at this coffee. This dirty-looking stuff in the tin cup is coffee. It is not French drip coffee. You can't taste the coffee in it. You can taste the saltpetre in it, though. It is lousy with this taste of saltpetre. They douse it with this stuff to help you be a good Christian. That is thoughtful of them.

I finish this stuff and go out in the chapel. You get no flop in this mission unless you listen to the sermon. For seven nights a week I have to listen to a sermon. They are long sermons. Sermons that last for three hours. This chapel is a big room. It is filled with stiffs waiting for their flop. Around the walls are religious pictures in fancy colors. It is warm in here. It is damp and chilly in the parks, but it is warm in here.

WAITING FOR NOTHING

They have a woman preacher tonight. She stands in the pulpit and waves her arms and jumps up and down. She is going strong. Her voice is like a rasp that grates on your nerves. She is burning up. The sweat pours down her face. She is whooping it up because she is on her favorite subject. She is preaching about getting washed in the blood of the Lamb. They always preach about getting washed in the blood of the Lamb. I am sick of all this. I have heard it so many times.

Now, that girl on the left in the choir is not bad-looking. She looks nice sitting up there with her pink dress, and the violets pinned to her waist. She is too damn good-looking to be wasting her time in this joint. She is daffy like the rest of them, though. She must be daffy, or she would not be in this joint trying to get a bunch of stiffs to get washed in the blood of the Lamb.

This woman preacher has been giving these stiffs plenty of hell, and now she is getting ready to hand out the old soft soap.

"The trouble with you dear men is that you are away from the blessed saving power of Jesus Christ," she says. "You got to get washed in the blood of the Lamb. Only Christ can make you clean. Won't you come up and give your hearts to Christ tonight? Everything will be yours. Peace will be yours. Peace and calm will come into your

45

souls. You will be new men. Christ can give you what you want. Is it a job you want? Christ can give you a job. Ask and you shall receive. How many men will come up to the altar tonight and give their hearts to Christ? Hold up your hands."

We do not hold up our hands. We are old-timers. We have tried this stunt before. Once in Denver I kneeled at the mourners' bench till I had blisters on my knees. I prayed for a job. I thought for sure I'd get me a job. Well, sister, I didn't get any job. I got throwed in their lousy can for sleeping in the park. No, we cannot fall for that stuff. We are old-timers. We are on to your little tricks.

"Will every man in the house bow his head while we ask the blessing of God upon each of you dear, unfortunate men? Let every head be bowed in the presence of the Lord. I see some men in the rear of the room reading newspapers. Put your newspapers away, men. This is no place to be reading of temporal things. You know, men, that is just the trouble with us today. We are too much taken up with worldly things. If we could just get back to God and let the blessed Savior have His way with us, our troubles would vanish like the driven snow. Let every head in the house of God be bowed. Thank you, men."

We bow our heads. We know better than not to bow our heads. We've seen too many stiffs get

kicked out in the cold because they didn't bow
their heads. We are sick of this drivel this dame is
handing out, but it is warm in here. It is cold outside.

"Now, men, while every head is bowed and
every heart is lifted, how many of you men would
like to have us pray for you? You don't have to
come up in front. You don't even have to stand
on your feet. Just raise your hand if you would
like to have us pray for you. Some of you men have
hearts so heavy with burdens you can hardly bear
them. Many of you dear souls are standing on the
brink of despair, and some even on the brink of
eternity. Oh, brother, we know One who will de-
liver you from the darkness. We know One who
will fill that sick heart of yours with new life and
new hope. Raise your hands so we will know who
to pray for. God hears and answers prayer."

It is the same old stuff. I can see that it is the
same old stuff. She is leading them up slow. This
is only the first step. Some of these stiffs who are
new to this are going to find themselves kneeling
up there at the mourners' bench, and wondering
how they got up there.

"Raise your hands men," she says. "Just raise
your hands. You don't have to come up in front."

Fifteen or twenty raise their hands. They want
to be prayed for. I raise my hand. The more hands

47

that are raised, the sooner she will quit harping. She is running true to form tonight. She makes the next step.

"Thank God there are so many men realize the healing power of Jesus Christ. You men who raised your hands, how many of you have the courage to stand up on your feet? I tell you, men, it takes courage to stand up on your feet in the presence of your fellow men, unafraid, and ask God to help you. Some of you men haven't got that courage. How many will stand up and ask God to help you?"

It is the same old stuff. She is soft-soaping them now.

"Come on, men," she says, "who will stand up first for Jesus Christ?"

Some mission stiff in the front row stands up. That's what he's here in the front row for, to lead the lambs to slaughter. Come back here in a year, and you will find this same mission stiff standing up and asking God to help him. As much as these guys ask for help, you'd think they'd get a little help sometimes.

"I am always ready to stand up for the Lord," this mission stiff says.

A couple of young punks stand up. They don't know what it's all about. They feel like I did that time in Denver when I wore blisters on my knees.

Pretty soon there are ten standing up. Twenty raise their hands. Ten stand up. That's a pretty good average. This dame is pretty good. She is going strong. She has got them where she wants them. They are standing up.

"Now you men that are standing on your feet, just come up here to the altar. I want to give every one of you a Bible. I want you to study God's word. I want you to know God."

She holds out the Bibles to them. They are standing up. It is easier to go up and get the Bible than to sit back down in their seats while she is holding them out to them. She has got them where she wants them. They march up front and take this paper-backed book. It is not a Bible. It's just one book of the Bible. I know. I've got plenty of them. I was new then. I am an old-timer now. They don't get me to stand up on my feet to be prayed for any more. These stiffs take these books and start back towards their seats. But they don't get away with this stuff. Who do they think they are to get away with this stuff?

"Just a minute, men," she says. "I'd like to ask God's special blessing on each of you dear brothers tonight. Won't you kneel at the altar for just a few seconds?"

These guys stop in their tracks and look funny. They don't know what to do. Well, what can they

do? Kneel at the altar, that's all they can do. She
didn't get them up here to give them a paper-
backed book. She got them up here to kneel. They
kneel.

"Let us pray," she says.

She starts to pray. When she starts to pray, all
the choir and the mission stiffs gather around the
mourners' bench. They put their arms around
these guys that are roped at the altar, and start
working on them to give their hearts to God. The
young punk on the end of the bench is lucky. He
draws the girl in the pink dress with the violets
pinned to her waist. I do not blame that guy if he
gives his heart to God. For five, ten minutes nobody
gives their heart to God. These guys start to squirm
on their knees. This mourners' bench hasn't got
any soft rug to kneel on. These mission guys are
smart. They make you so miserable you will give
your heart to God so you can get up off your knees.
Pretty soon some guy can't stand it any longer. I
see him shake his head. This mission stiff who has
his arm around him gets to his feet. He has a grin
on his map a yard wide. The punk gets up, too.
His knees are all in. He can hardly stand up.

"Praise God," this mission stiff yells, "the lamb
was lost, but now he is found."

He shakes hands with the punk.

Everybody shakes hands with the punk.

"Amen," shouts the red-headed woman with the big legs.

"Glory to God!" somebody yells back.

The skinny woman at the organ begins playing a hymn. She is glory-bound. She slams down on the keys with all her might. She wiggles her shoulders and throws her head back. There is a wild look in her eyes. She jumps off the stool and starts dancing a jig. She keeps time with the clapping of her hands. Everyone else starts clapping their hands.

This woman preacher watches this organ-player dance and keeps time by pounding her foot on the floor. Christ, but she's happy. She has got these guys where she wants them. She raises her hand in the air.

"What did all the people say?" she yells at the choir and the mission stiffs.

"All the people said amen," they yell back.

One by one the rest of these stiffs that are roped at the mourners' bench get to their feet. It's hell on your knees to stay there for half an hour.

"Brother, do you give your heart to God?" shouts this woman preacher to the stiff with the purple birthmark on his face.

He shakes his head yes, he gives his heart to God.

"Though your sins be as scarlet, He can make them white as snow," she yells.

She claps her hands together. She has got these stiffs where she wants them.

"Praise God. Washed in the blood," yells one of these mission stiffs. "God will take care of you. Whatever you need, God will give it to you."

"I need a shave," pipes up this stiff in the third row. "Am I next?"

This mission stiff sputters. This woman preacher does not sputter. She walks to the edge of the pulpit and points her finger at this stiff.

"Brother," she says, "the Devil has got you. The Devil is living in your soul. We want nothing to do with the Devil here. Beat it."

This guy grins and goes out. It will be the park bench for him. It don't pay to talk back to a mission stiff.

"Praise God, men," she says, "the Devil is now out of this house. The house of the Lord is no place for Satan. All evening I have felt his presence here. I tell you men, when you get close to Jesus Christ, when you have touched the hem of His garment, you can feel the Devil when he's in the same room with you. You can look into people's eyes and see him. I can see him in some of your eyes now. Oh, sinners, won't you run him out and come up to the mourners' bench?"

Nobody runs the Devil out.

All these guys that went up to the mourners'

bench line up and march upstairs. They do not
sleep with us sinners. They have been washed in
the blood. They sleep in the converts' room. There
are clean sheets on the beds of the converts' room.
They are not lousy. A stiff who wears blisters on
his knees at the mourners' bench deserves a good,
clean flop.

This woman preacher wipes the sweat off her
face and sits down. She has had a hard night's work.
A mission stiff in a purple suit and a pair of red
suspenders takes her place in the pulpit.

It is time to testify. After the preaching it is
time to testify.

"How many of you men would like to stand up
and tell what God has done for you?" yells this mission stiff.

These stiffs are in this joint because they have
no place to get in out of the cold, and this bastard
asks them to stand up and tell what God has done
for them. I can tell him what God has done for
them. He hasn't done a damn thing for them. I
don't though. It is warm in here. It is cold outside.

Another mission stiff gets up. You can always
depend on a mission stiff telling what God has done
for him.

"For twenty years I was a dope fiend—"

For Christ's sake, won't someone knock this hop-
head back in his seat? Every night I have to listen

to this guy. Every night he adds a little bit extra. But then maybe you can't blame this crazy slop-swiller. Every guy likes to shine a little bit. Testifying is the only chance he has. Maybe you can't blame this guy for getting up and saying for twenty years he was a dope fiend. When he gets up, he is good for half an hour. He knows he is fixed for half an hour. You can't make a guy sit down when he is telling what Jesus Christ has done for him.

"I just couldn't get along without my shot of snow," he says. "I couldn't sleep, and I couldn't work or eat. Brethren, the Devil had such a hold on me that I wished I was dead. One rainy night I was crouched all alone in my room. I was just a twitchin' all over. I was out of dope. I just felt as though if I didn't get me some dope, I would go daffy. 'Satan,' I said, 'by the grace of God, I am goin' to lick you.' I pulled out my old dust-covered Bible that had been layin' there in the desk since my angel mother passed over to her reward. I made myself set down at the table and read it. I read for an hour before I closed the good book up. 'Now then, Satan,' I says, 'you and me are goin' to fight it out.' Well, sir, we wrestled there all night, me and Satan. First he would be on top, and then me. Along about mornin' when the sky was gettin' gray in the east, and Satan just about had me licked, I looked out of the window. Brethren, what I am tellin' you is the God's truth. There, lookin' into the window was the face of Jesus Christ, just as plain as that picture of Him on the wall. I see Him look into my eyes pitying like, and I saw His lips move. 'Satan,' He says, 'this is no child of yours, this is My child. Son, your sins are forgiven. Come into My service.' Well, sir, from that day on, I have never touched a pinch of dope. Praise God, blessed be the name of the Lord!"

He sits down. No one else gets up. Even the mission stiffs are too fagged out to tell what God has done for them. We stand up. This woman preacher says the benediction. We march upstairs to the third floor. Most of these stiffs pull off their clothes and crawl into these dirty blankets. Some of them go in to wash. I go in to wash, myself.

I notice this guy in the gray suit. He is a middle-aged guy. He has not been on the fritz long. I can tell. Up and down, back and forth he walks. He is plenty nervous about something. He does not pay any attention to the rest of these stiffs. He walks from one end of the room to the other. His eyes are glued to the floor. I know what he is thinking. I have walked like that myself. Up and down through the night.

"She is a tough life, buddy," I say.

He does not look up. He does not answer. A nice friendly guy.

"She will all come out in the wash," I say.

"Yeah," he says, "she will all come out in the wash."

He walks into one of these toilets and closes the door. I go on with my washing. I do not think any more about this guy. All at once a roar comes out of that toilet. Smoke curls up over the door. I know what caused that roar. A gun caused that roar. That damn fool has shot himself. That is plain. I run over to the door and try to open it. It is locked from the inside. The stiffs are pouring into this toilet now. They have heard the shot. I get down on my hands and knees and look through the crack in the door.

"What do you see?" some stiff says.

"Plenty," I say.

I am sick in the stomach when I get up. I have seen all I want to see. This guy is sprawled out on the floor with a hole in his head. It is a jagged hole. There is a pool of blood on the floor. His arm is folded up under his head. Some of the blood drips in his hand and runs down the sleeve of his coat. Some of this blood is darker than the rest. That is not blood. That is his brains. This guy is stone dead, all right. His eyes are wide open.

"What's he wanna bump hisself off fer?" says this stiff with the boils on his face. "There ain't nothin' to bump yerself off fer."

"He bumped hisself off because he's got the guts to bump hisself off," says this other stiff. "We are afraid to bump ourselves off, so we live in mission flops and guzzle lousy mission slop."

Somebody has called an ambulance. This stiff does not need an ambulance. He needs a hearse. They run us all out into the hall. We huddle in a bunch and wait to see them carry this stiff out. They bring him out with a sheet spread over him. It is a clean sheet. It came from the converts' room. This is the first time this stiff has had a clean sheet over him for a long time.

I go back to my room and sit on the edge of my bed. It is cold sitting here, but I do not mind the cold. I am thinking about bumping myself off. Why not? It don't hurt. I bet that guy never knew what hit him. Just a jagged hole, and a pool of blood mixed with black, and it is all over. He had the guts, and now everything is all right with him. After a guy bumps himself off, he don't have any more troubles. Everything is all right with him.

I walk over to the window. Down below me is the alley, but I cannot see it. The glass of the window is covered with fly specks, and besides, it is dark and murky down there. It is a long way to the bottom. It is three stories to the bottom. Three stories, with a nice concrete pavement to light on. If a guy was to jump head-first out of this window, it would be all over. Just a few seconds, and it would be all over. I think of that blood splotched with black on the toilet floor. I think of me sprawled on the pavement in the blackness of the alley below.

"Messy," I think, "messy and gooey."

I pull off my clothes and crawl into bed.

CHAPTER FOUR

It is evening. I sit on this park bench and watch the people as they pass. A guy comes down the walk. He twists and wiggles with mincing steps. His eyelashes are mascara'd, and his cheeks are rouged. His lips are flaming red with lipstick. He sits down on this bench beside me. He is perfumed plenty, and he smells pretty good.

"Oho," I think, "this guy is queer, and he doesn't care who knows it."

He pulls out a gold cigarette case and puts a cigarette between his lips. I notice that the lipstick dyes the end of it red. He reaches in his pocket and fumbles for a match. He knows he hasn't got a match. I know he hasn't got a match. We are playing a game.

"Got a match, deary?" he says.

"Sure." I give him a match.

"Care for a smoke?"

I take a cigarette. It is a high-class cigarette. You will not find any like it lying over the curbs. It has a cork tip.

"It's certainly nice in the park this evening," he says.

He purses up his lips and hums like a bird.

"Nicer than last night," I say. "I slept on this bench last night."

This fairy already knows I am on the fritz, but this will make sure he knows it.

"Awful cold?"

"Cold as hell."

"No covers?"

"Newspapers. Newspapers are warm, but the cold comes up through the cracks in the bench."

"That is awful," he says.

"Yeah, it sure is tough," I say.

"How do you eat?"

He knows how I eat, but we are playing a game.

"I eat wherever I can," I say. "Sometimes I get a hand-out from a house. Sometimes a cup of coffee from a restaurant."

"You poor dear," he says. "It must be terrible to live like that."

"What can a guy do?" I say. "A guy has got to live."

"Why, I should think you would be skin and bones," he says.

He lays his hand across my leg. I must not jerk my leg away. He is feeling me out. If I jerk my leg away, he will see that he is not going to make me. This queer will not put out for a meal until he sees that I am a good risk. I leave my knee where it is. These pansies give me the willies, but I have got to get myself a feed. I have not had a decent feed for a week.

"I am not so skinny," I say.

This guy motions around the park.

"Everyone seems to have a girl," he says.

"You have to have dough to get a girl," I say. "Girls are expensive. If you haven't got any dough, you haven't got any girl."

"Did you ever have a girl?" he says.

"Sure, I had a girl," I say, "but I lost my dough, so I lost my girl."

"A good-looking fellow like you ought to get a girl without any money," he says.

He pinches my leg.

I feel the goose-pimples on my leg and the shivers on my back. A pansy like this, with his plucked eyebrows and his rouged lips, is like a snake to me. I am afraid of him. Why I am afraid of this fruit with his spindly legs and his flat chest, I do not know.

"Not so you can notice it," I say. "Girls want the dough."

"Well, sometimes two fellows can have a pretty good time together," he says. "Did you ever go out with any fellows?"

"I never did," I say.

I am lying, but if this queer wants a virgin, that's what he gets.

"I bet you and I could have a wonderful time together," he says. "When two people get to know each other real well, they find they have just a lot in common."

"That's right," I say.

"What are you doing tonight?" he says.

"Not a thing," I say.

"How would you like to go to a good show tonight?"

"I would like that fine, but hell—" I look down at my seedy clothes, and my shoes without soles.

"I can fix you up with clothes," he says. "I have a friend about your size. I will get some from him."

"That will be fine," I say.

"And a bath," he says; "you will feel better after

62

a good warm bath. I have a bath in mauve tile in my apartment. You will feel better after a good warm bath."

His eyes sparkle when he mentions the bath. He licks his lips. I notice that he smears the lipstick when he licks his lips. He takes hold of the end of my belt and fingers it.

"That is a nice belt you have on," he says. "That belt must have cost plenty of money when it was new."

My belt is a cheap belt. It cost two bits when it was new. It is old and frayed at the edges now, but we are playing a game.

"It is a pretty good belt," I say.

He starts to unfasten it. There are people here. They will see him. I pull away. He notices that I pull away. He lets go of my belt.

"Can you meet me here tonight at eight o'clock?" he says.

"Sure, I'll meet you here," I say.

He pulls four bits out of his pocket. He has decided I am a good risk.

"This is for your dinner," he says.

"Thanks," I say. "You are all right."

He pulls out a mirror and straightens the lipstick on his lips.

"Gracious me," he says, "I am a total wreck." He gets up. "Well, deary, don't forget. Toodle-doo

63

until tonight." He wiggles down the walk.

I am a lucky stiff running into this queer. For every queer there is a hundred stiffs to make him. It is seven o'clock. I have an hour to wait. I walk over to this hash-house across the street and order me a beef stew. This joint smells like a slop-jar, but the grub is cheap and hits the spot.

"Did you make her?" this skinny stiff next to me at the counter says.

"Make who?" I say.

"Mrs. Carter," he says. "I see you talkin' to her in the park."

"So her name is Mrs. Carter?" I say. "Sure, I made her for four bits. I got a date for tonight."

"You better fill it. She's in the dough. Lousy with it."

"Any strings on her?"

"Not now. She was livin' with a stiff she picked up off the street, but Geraldine, that big red-headed guy with the scarred face, took him away from her."

"How did Mrs. Carter like that?" I say.

"Mrs. Carter says that Geraldine is a two-timing bitch. She says that if Geraldine didn't look so much like a wolf, she would pull her hair out by the roots."

"Will she treat a guy right?" I say.

"She will treat a guy swell," he says, "if she

64

likes him. You are a lucky stiff making Mrs. Carter. There are plenty of stiffs in this town would give their eye teeth to make Mrs. Carter."

"Where does she hang out?"

"She lives up on the Avenue with the swells. The joint she lives in is lousy with queers, and what is more, they are lousy with jack. Mrs. Carter rooms with a cashier of a bank."

"He queer, too?" I say.

"Sure, she's queer," he says, "but you will not have a chance with her. Mrs. Carter would cut your throat if you tried to pull the wool over her eyes. She is a tough customer. She says she will scratch Geraldine's eyes out does she get the chance. My advice is stick to Mrs. Carter."

I finish my beef stew and go back to the park. There are more people here now. The benches are full. They loll on the grass. It is dark. Every other guy is a queer. The other guy is trying to make her. They twist down the walk. They ogle the guys that pass as they sit on the benches. They wink at the prospects.

An old guy sits on the bench across from me. He is as queer as they make them. He keeps ogling at me. I do not pay him any attention. He purses up his lips. He clucks through his teeth like an old hen.

"Missus," I think, "you are wasting your time.

WAITING FOR NOTHING

I am waiting for my meal ticket. I am waiting for
Mrs. Carter. Mrs. Carter rooms with a cashier of
a bank, and what is more, she is lousy with jack
herself."

I cannot be bothered with an old queer who
clucks through his teeth like a hen.

It is a good thing I am not flirting with this old
guy, for I spot Mrs. Carter frisking down the walk.
The stiffs are winking as she passes. They whistle
low. They cannot whistle loud. The coppers will
hear them. The coppers will let you whistle low,
but not loud. She does not pay them any attention.
She breezes straight up to the bench where I am
sitting.

"Right on the dot, deary," she croons. "Your glad
rags are waiting at the apartment."

I get up. The rest of these stiffs scowl at me. They
are jealous. We walk down the street. We are going
to this fairy's room. It is misery for me to walk on
the street with this queer. People stop in their
tracks and watch her wiggle. They look at her
rouged lips and her plucked eyebrows. They laugh.

"Oh ho," they say, "she has got a beau."

I turn my eyes to the ground and try not to pay
any attention. What the hell? This guy is my meal
ticket. I will go right along to his room. I wish
we were there now, though. I do not like to have
people winking at me. Maybe they will think I am

queer, too. I'd like to see some bastard accuse me of being queer. The first guy that calls me a pansy, it will be just too bad for that guy. That guy will never call anyone else a pansy.

We are getting into the ritzy section. There are big apartments on this street. It will cost plenty of jack to pay rent on one of these joints. I can see that this guy is in the big dough, all right. We turn into the one with the red marquee in front. The floor of the hall is covered with blue tile. There are marble statues, and paintings that are real paintings on the walls. This is some joint, all right. We take the elevator. The elevator boy grins at this queer. I bet this guy is one of his best customers. I bet this guy will make this queer, himself. This is a funny world, and there are a lot of funny people in it. That is one thing I have learned since I have been on the road.

We walk down the hall and stop before room 22. He opens the door. I follow him in. My mouth pops open when I stand inside. Never have I seen such a classy lay-out. The walls are black. The ceiling is black, black satin that hangs in folds to the floor. It is a big room, a big room like a room in a palace. A chandelier of glass stretches from the ceiling. It hangs from bronze chains. The links are as big around as my wrist. My shoes sink far down into this thick, gray rug. My shabby shoes without soles do not belong on such a rug as this.

There is another guy sprawled out on a sky-blue lounge. I can see that this guy is queer, too. He is decked out in a peach negligee. It is edged in gold. He crosses his legs as he reads. There is no hair on them. They are shaved. On one of his ankles is a bracelet, a silver bracelet. On it is a pink cameo as big as an egg.

"Have a good date, deary?" he says without looking up from his book.

"Look for yourself," Mrs. Carter says.

This guy looks up, and squeals when he sees me. He jerks his negligee down over his legs like a woman would do, and jumps up.

"Stay right where you are, deary," Mrs. Carter says, "this is my date. Meet my room-mate, Gloria," she says to me. "She is cashier in a bank."

"How do you do?" I say.

Gloria does not answer. She is sulking at Mrs. Carter. She lies stomach-down on the lounge and pretends she is reading. She is not reading. She is only pretending.

"Wait here until I change my rags," Mrs. Carter says to me.

She goes into the bedroom and closes the door. Gloria winks at me and squenches up her nose at Mrs. Carter in the bedroom. I do not pay her any attention. I remember what the stiff in the hashhouse told me. I cannot take any chances. Those nails of Mrs. Carter's, sharp-pointed and painted a flaming red, were meant for something. I do not wish to have my eyes scratched out.

"Come and sit by me," she whispers.

I shake my head no.

"Afraid of her?" she says. "She couldn't hurt a flea."

She speaks low, but I am afraid Mrs. Carter will hear. I do not answer.

"You are blond," she says, "and Mrs. Carter is blond. You do not go together. I am brunette. My hair is wavy. Mrs. Carter's is straight."

She tosses her head to show me her hair is wavy.

"I come here with Mrs. Carter," I say. "She bought me a meal. What can I do?"

"I will buy you plenty of meals, deary," she says, "better meals than she will buy you. How would you like to have a new suit? Your clothes are shabby. How would a new suit be?"

"A new suit would be fine," I say. "I could use a new suit."

"What color do you like?" she says.

"Gray," I say. "I like a double-breasted gray suit with two pants."

"You would look good in a gray suit," she says; "a gray suit would be the thing. I will get you one tomorrow."

"What about Mrs. Carter?" I say.

"Mrs. Carter?" she says. "Who cares about Mrs. Carter. She is an old hag."

"She might hear you in the other room," I say. She lowers her voice.

"Do you know how old Mrs. Carter is?" she says.

"No," I say, "I don't know."

"Twenty-eight, that's how old. Twenty-eight. If she didn't wear the war paint like a common whore, she'd look fifty."

"You don't use much paint," I say.

"I do not have to use much paint," she says, "I am only twenty-three. When I look as old as Mrs. Carter, I will shoot myself."

"You do not even look twenty-three," I say.

"Do you know what Mrs. Carter will do to you when she is through with you?" she says.

"No," I say. "What will she do?"

"She will kick you out in the cold, that is what she will do. I see her kick plenty of her beaux out in the cold. When she is through, she is through. Now, I like you. I would never kick you out in the cold. You can stay with me as long as you want. I like you a lot. I will take better care of you than Mrs. Carter."

The bedroom door opens. Mrs. Carter comes in. She is wearing a black nightgown that is made of silk.

"You will have to sleep on the lounge tonight, Gloria," she says.

Gloria does not answer. She is burned up.

"Come on in the bedroom," Mrs. Carter says to me.

I follow her in. She makes a face at Gloria as she closes the door.

"She is a cat," she says, "a jealous, two-faced cat."

I sit down on the lounge. She sits down beside me. We are not going to a show. I can see that. That was only a gag.

"Nice place you have here," I say. "I have never seen a classier place." I have to say something.

"Yes, it's nice," she says. "I'm glad you like it. You can stay here for a long time if you want to."

She moves up closer to me and puts her arm over the back of the lounge. Her fingers touch my neck. I feel the cold chills go up my back. I pull away.

She frowns.

"What's the matter?" she says. "Don't you like me?"

"Sure, I like you," I say.

"You don't act like it," she says.

"Well," I say, "a guy likes to get acquainted a little bit first. Sure, I like you fine, but a guy likes to wait a little first."

"Don't you think I'm pretty?" she says.

"Sure, you're pretty," I say. "You're a good-looking guy, all right."

She frowns again.

"I am not a guy," she says.

"Well," I say, "you're a good-looking—you're a good-looking girl."

"As good-looking as Gloria?"

"Better, a lot better than Gloria."

"She is a slut," she says, "a no-good, double-crossing slut. She would take you away from me if she could. Could she?"

"Her?" I say. "Not her. She hasn't got a chance. I just can't see Gloria."

I am ashamed of all this. I am sick in the stomach, I am so ashamed of all this. What can I do? What I am doing is all I can do. A stiff has got to live.

"What did she say about me in there?" she says.

"Nothing," I say. "She didn't say nothing."

"She said something. I heard her mention my name. What did she say?"

"Oh, she said: 'How do you like Mrs. Carter?' That's all she said: 'How do you like Mrs. Carter?' "

"What did you tell her?"

" 'Fine,' I said. 'I like her fine.' "

"Did you just say that or did you mean it?"

"I meant it. Sure, I meant it."

72

"Were you ever in love with anyone? Did you ever have a girl?"

"Sure, I was in love. Sure, I had a girl. I told you in the park I used to have a girl. But I haven't any girl now. I haven't got any dough. No dough, no girl."

"Are you still in love with her?" she says.

"Well," I say, "what good would it do me? What good would it do a stiff if he was in love with his girl? When a guy loses his job in his home town, he has to go on the fritz. He has to grab himself a drag out of town. A guy can't be dinging back doors for hand-outs and flopping behind signboards when his girl lives in the next block."

"I don't want you to have a girl," she says; "I want you to stay here."

"That is nice of you," I say.

"You won't have to worry about eating here. You won't have to sleep behind signboards, either. I have a nice bed."

Her eyes sparkle when she looks at her bed. It is an oak bed. An oak bed with sky-blue spreads, and pillow slips of silk.

She gets up and crawls into the bed.

"Come on to bed," she says.

"In a little bit," I say.

"It is cold out there. It is nice and warm in here," she says.

WAITING FOR NOTHING

I want to put this off as long as possible. But not this guy. He wants to go to bed. He will not talk any more. He yawns.

"I can't sleep with the light on," he says. "Come on to bed."

It is chilly here, and I am sleepy. I will have to go to bed some time. This queer will stay awake until I do go to bed. What the hell? A guy has got to eat, and what is more, he has got to flop.

"Sure," I say, "I am ready for the hay."

You can always depend on a stiff having to pay for what he gets. I pull off my clothes and crawl into bed.

CHAPTER FIVE

IT IS afternoon, and I have not eaten today. I press my hand over this bulge in my coat pocket, and watch this stiff who stands on the corner. I can see that he is going to eat, and he does not need a bulge in his coat pocket to do it, either. He does not need to risk getting a copper's bullet in his guts. He walks over to this skinny guy with the girl on his arm.

"Buddy," he says, "could you spare a little change to help a hungry man get something to eat?"

This skinny guy with the girl on his arm stops and scowls at this stiff. He does not want to part

75

with his change to help a hungry man get something
to eat.

"Why don't you get a job and go to work?" he
says.

"There ain't no work," this stiff says. "I can't
find no work anywhere."

"I ain't got no money for bums," this guy says.

"Go on," this girl says, "give him some dough.
Maybe he is hungry. Times is pretty tough."

"They sure are tough, lady," this stiff says.

This skinny guy growls. He does not care if times
are tough or not. His belly is full. He is sitting on
top of the world. He has a good-looking girl hanging on his arm. What is a hungry stiff to him?
He wants to tell this stiff to get the hell out of his
sight, but he can't do that. That would not make
a hit with this girl. There is only one thing he can
do. Shell out, that's all he can do. This stiff is smart.
He knows that's all this guy can do. He has got this
guy where he wants him. It must feel pretty good
to have one of these bastards where you want him.

He reaches down in his pocket and pulls out two
bits. He would like to pull out a jitney, but he
can't do that. This girl is looking. He does not
want to look like a cheap skate in front of his girl.
A jitney or a ten-cent piece does not go with a girl.
She knows a stiff cannot fill up his belly on a ten-
cent piece.

"Thank you," this stiff says. "Thank you, and the lady."

He slouches down the street.

This skinny guy grunts. He does not like parting with his dough.

I admire that stiff. He has got the guts. He does not need to go with a gnawing pain in his belly. I do not need to go with a pain in my belly, either. I have not got the guts to hit me a guy with a girl, but I have got the guts to hit a high-toned restaurant. If I cannot get me a feed in this restaurant, I have got the bulge in my pocket. I am tired of having the pain in my guts. I have made up my mind. This is the last time I will whine for a feed. I am going to show these bastards I will get mine. That is why I have the bulge that I cover up with my hand.

I walk into this joint and stand by the cash register. I look around. I have hit me some high-toned joints, but never one such as this. There are no counters here. Only tables. Women sit at these tables. It is not evening, but they have on evening gowns. On their feet are gold and silver slippers. They glitter with the jewels that are on their fingers and arms. The men are sporting coats with tails. The tables sparkle with the shine of silver dishes. I stand there, and I cannot imagine people living like this. I cannot believe it.

They look up from their tables and stare at me. I do not blame them. I am a crummy-looking customer to be in a joint like this. I know that. But I am here. I am after something to eat. I am going to get something to eat, too, or know the reason why.

"What do you want?" this cashier says.

She has a hard face. She is not going to be friendly. I can see that.

"I want to see the manager," I say.

"What do you want with the manager?" she says.

"Private business," I say.

This manager is standing at one of the tables. He sees me talking to the cashier and comes over.

"What do you want?" he says.

"I want something to eat," I say. "I am a hungry man."

All these customers can hear me asking for something to eat. It will not do this manager's business any good to turn down a hungry man for something to eat. He knows that. I know he knows it. That's why I am in this classy joint.

He grins and slaps me on the back.

"Sure, I can give a hungry man something to eat," he says. "Come on back in the kitchen with me."

All these cash customers grin. This manager's all right, they think. We will eat here regular. He

78

deserves our trade. He will feed a hungry man. I can see where this guy is all right, too. I can see where I am going to get a high-class feed. Well, I need a high-class feed. We walk back to the kitchen.

This manager closes the door to the kitchen so these cash customers cannot hear.

"Hey, Fritz," he yells, "give this bum a cup of coffee and send him out the back way."

The lousy bastard. A cup of coffee. Out there he slapped me on the back. He was all smiles out there. He was showing off. I would like to take a sock at this guy, but I cannot. I cannot take any chances on getting pinched while I have the bulge in my pocket.

I walk out the back way without waiting on this coffee.

All right, I think, all right. We will not hit any more restaurants. We will not whine for any more feeds. We will either get it or we won't get it. I walk down the street. I keep my hand in my right coat pocket. There is not so much of a bulge when my hand is there. They will think it is only my hand. But it is not my hand. I have a gat in this pocket. It is heavy and black. It is a good gat. It will shoot straight. It will shoot straight if I can keep my hand from shaking, and I will have to keep my hand from shaking. I will not be caught. I have thought it all out. I have spent the night thinking it all out. I have made up my mind. Before I will be caught, I will shoot. And I will shoot straight. If I cannot get away, if they corner me, just one of these little slugs will be enough for me. My troubles will be over. I will not have any more to worry about. They have starved me to death long enough. I am tired of walking the streets all day long asking for work. They laugh at you for asking for work.

"There is no work," they say. "We cannot keep the men we have. If it's a meal you want, you can go to the mission. You can get a good meal at the mission."

I will stop asking for work. I will quit standing in the soup-lines for hours for a bowl of slop. I have made up my mind to take a chance. You can only die once.

I finger this gat. I have waited a long time to get my fingers on a gat like this. At night, on the cold ground in the jungles, I have dreamed about a gat like this. Blue black. A gat that will shoot straight. A gat that will not miss. Now I have it. The stiff I stole this gat from was drunk. He does not need this gat. He will be soused up for a week. Maybe in a week I will give him back his gat, and a wad of dough besides.

I walk on down the street. It is clogged with people. They do not look at me, and if they do, they do not see me. They do not notice my ragged clothes, and my beard that I have let grow for a week. They have troubles of their own. Some of these guys I pass on the street are wishing to Christ they could get their fingers on a gat. Well, I have my fingers on a gat. They are around the handle now. It is a good handle. It is not smooth and shiny like the rest of the gat, but rough. It is rough so you can get a good grip on it. It will not slip out of your hands.

I have planned it all out. There must be no hitch in my planning. In my pocket is my razor. After I have pulled this job and got away, I will shave. You would not know I am the same guy when I have shaved. I will have plenty of dough in my kick, too. Stacks of dough like these tellers have in their wire cages in the banks. That will make me a different guy.

It is time I got down the street. I know the time. I have picked the best time. I have had my fingers on this gat for two days now. I have been figuring during those two days. I know what I am doing. I know just what to do. This cop will be passing that joint now. There is a box on the corner. He will be reporting. He will not be back for an hour. Well, an hour will make lots of difference. There's lots can happen in an hour. In an hour I will be a rich man. I will be a rich man or

I will be stretched out on a marble slab in the morgue.

I stop across the street. This is not a big bank. It is a branch bank. I know better than to try to hold up a big bank. I know what I am doing. I am not crazy. I am not a fool. I look across through the window. There are men in white shirts working in there. Their sleeves are rolled up. It is hot in there. I watch them as they pass out these bills to the line of customers in front of their windows. In the drawers in front of them are piles of bills. There are plenty of these piles. One or two of them will keep me for life. I will not have anything to worry about. I will be fixed for life. What have I got to lose? Nothing. What have I got to live for? Soup and stale bread, that is what I have to live for. That is what I have to lose.

I have thought it all out. There is an alley a little ways from this bank. It leads to several short streets. There is a barrel in the rear of one of these stores in the alley. In this barrel I will throw my gat and my coat and hat. I will walk out on one of these short streets. Up the street a little ways there is a picture show. I will go in. I will not hand the ticket girl one of these bills that I get in the bank. That might give me away. I am taking no chances. I have a two-bit piece in my pants pocket for that. There must not be any slip. I will stay in this show while they are hunting for me. I will shave in the toilet. At night I will come out. I will not hang around the streets. I will go to the mission. They will never look for me in the mission. The last place in the world they will look for a guy with plenty of jack will be the mission. I will not spend any money in this town. I will stay in this mission as long as they will let me. Then I will leave town, but it will be on no drag with its hard, cold box cars I will leave on. I will leave on a passenger, and it will not be on the blinds with the roar of the wind, and the sound of the wheels underneath me. It will be on the cushions.

I press my hand over my pocket to cover up this bulge and walk across the street and into the bank. To the left are the writing-tables. Two women are writing checks. To the right are the bank guys' cages. There are five windows here. Through each one I can see a guy dishing out money. I go up to one of these tables and let on like I am writing a check. I am not writing a check. I am seeing if the coast is clear. I have always wondered how a guy felt when he was robbing a bank. Now I know. I am getting ready to stick up this bank myself. I cannot imagine me holding up a bank. I know how these guys felt now. I know the sickish feeling they had in the pit of their bellies. I know the jerky shake of their hands. I am not going to weaken

now. I have made up my mind. Shaky hands or
not, I will sleep in no more lousy mission flops.
I have whined for my last meal. I have the gat and
I am going to use it if I have to. No one cares
whether I live or die. They would let me starve to
death on the streets without lifting a hand to help
me. Why should I care about these guys that hand
out these piles of bills from their wire cages? What
are they to me? If I stemmed one of these guys on
the street, he would tell me to get the hell out of
his sight before he called a cop. To hell with everybody. I am going to get mine.

I get in this line that waits in front of the first
cage. When I go out of here, I will have to do it
on the run. I do not want to run in front of any
more wire cages than I have to. They have got gats
themselves in those wire cages. It is not their dough,
but these bastards would take a pot shot at me just
to see me drop or maybe get a raise in pay. There
are five people standing in front of me. Two women
and three men. I stand behind this fat woman with
the big wrinkles in the back of her neck. She makes
a good screen. They cannot see me holding my
hand over this bulge that is in my coat pocket.
There are only two people in line at this next
cage, but I stay where I am. I want to be near the
door.

This line moves up slow. I have never seen a

line move so slow. You would think this was a soup-line it moves so slow. It is this fat woman's turn. She steps up to the window. I am right behind her. She shields me so that this guy in the cage in the white shirt-sleeves can hardly see me. At least he cannot see the bulge that is in my pocket. I glance sideways at this guy who is in the next cage. He is through with everyone in his line. He closes and locks this drawer with all the stacks of bills in it. He comes out of his cage and locks the door behind him. He goes into a room in the rear. That is a break for me. I will not have this guy taking pot shots at me from his cage, anyway. I put my hand in my pocket. I press my fingers tight around this gat. I feel the roughness of the handle. The roughness that is rough so that you can shoot it straight. I hope that I will not have to shoot straight. I hope that I will not have to shoot at all. My hand is shaking so. And my legs, too. I can feel them knocking against each other. It will not do to have my legs knocking against each other. My legs are what I am depending on to get me away from here fast.

This fat woman steps away from the window. I step up. I look at this guy. He looks at me.

"Yes, sir?" he says.

I do not say anything. I have nothing to say. I give this gat a yank, but it does not come out of my pocket. Only the handle comes out. Only the handle and a part of the lining of my coat. Something has happened. It is stuck in the torn lining of my pocket. I yank hard again, but it does not come out. This guy back of the wire cage thinks that there is something wrong. He steps closer to the window and peers out. He sees that my hand is in my pocket. He thinks there is something up. His face goes from pale to a sickish green. I know what that guy is feeling. I have the same feeling in the pit of my own belly. It is a sickish feeling, a vomity feeling. He takes a step back away from the window.

"What do you want?" he says. "What are you pulling at your pocket for?"

This guy is scared. He is plenty scared, but he has nothing on me. So am I.

"I have nothing in my pocket," I say. "Can't a guy put his hand in his pocket, if he wants to?"

I cannot take my hand out of my pocket. I am afraid he will see the bulge.

"What do you want?" he says. "What are you standing there pulling at your pocket for?"

"How much," I say, "how much does it take to start a checking account?"

"Twenty dollars," he says. "Twenty dollars."

He is not thinking what he is saying. His eyes are glued to my hand that is in my pocket. I cannot fool this guy with asking questions. He knows that there is something up. He does not take his eyes off my hand that is in my pocket. I cannot pull at this gat while he is looking. He will yell or set off the alarm. I can feel the cold sweat that stands out on my forehead. Christ, but I am scared. I have to get out of here, but how am I going to get out of here?

I turn around and start walking towards the door. I walk fast. I can feel this guy's eyes boring into the back of my head as I walk. I can feel the eyes of everyone that is in this bank on the bulge in my pocket that I cover up with my hand. I strain my ears waiting for the screech of the alarm. I wait to hear this guy yell for me to stop. I turn around and look back. This guy is backing out of his cage. His eyes never leave me. I see him there backing out of his cage, a pale, sickly look on his face. He is going after one of the cops that guard the bank. They must not catch me. They must not catch me with this bulge in my pocket that is the gat. I start to run. I shove this woman out of the way who is coming through the door. I swing round the doorway and hit up the street. The alley is what I want to reach. I must reach the alley before this cop gets to the street with his gat. I cannot have this cop filling me full of holes from behind. I run as fast as my shaking legs will carry me. I hear the slam of my feet on the sidewalk. I do not look back, but I can feel these people stop in their tracks and watch me run. I make it to this alley and the barrel round the corner. I do not stop here. I keep going. I run faster. Half-way up this alley, I glance back. No one has turned the corner yet. I spot this coal-chute that leads to the basement of one of these stores. I dive head-first into this and slide to the bottom. This basement has not been used for a long time. It is thick with cobwebs that stretch from the ceiling to the floor. They cover my face and get into my eyes as I clamber to the rafters from this box on the floor. These rafters are close together. I stretch myself out on them and lie quiet. There is only the sound of my gasping for breath as I lie here.

Outside, on the street, I imagine I can hear the voices of men yelling. I do not know if they are yelling about me or not. I do not even know if they are hunting for me or not. But I cannot forget that look in the teller's eyes as he looked at my hand in my coat pocket. I cannot forget the way he backed to the rear of the cage when he saw the bulge. He did not press the alarm. There was no alarm. I would have heard it if there was. If these guys outside are hunting for me, they are bastards. They would like to try what I tried, but they have not got the guts. They know they have not got the guts. That's why they are hunting for me. They have not got the guts to do what they want to do, so they are taking it out on a guy who has the guts.

I strain my ears for sounds in the alley outside, but there are none. But there are sounds on the street. I imagine I can hear the words "bank-robber." I crouch low on my rafters. I must not make a sound. Even if they crawl into the coal-chute, I must keep my head. I must lie still. I clutch this gat tighter in my hand. I must have it ready. If they come in here, they will have to have a light to see. When they flash that light on me, the guy that does it will not flash any more lights. He will be holding the light in his right hand. I will shoot to the left. But I will make sure. I will shoot once to the left and once to the right. I will show the bastards it does not pay to hunt for me. What do they know what is right and wrong? How can they know? They have not lived for years in lousy mission flops. They have not eaten swill from the restaurant garbage cans. They have good jobs. They do not know what is right or what is wrong.

I crouch here for hours. My body aches from every joint. The cramps shoot up my legs and up my back. The light that comes from the coal-chute grows from dim to pitch-dark. Outside it is night. There is no sound in the alley. Noises still come from the street. That noise would not be for me now. That is just the ordinary noise from the street. I think. Do not be a damn fool, I tell myself. They are not hunting for you. They were never hunting for you. There were plenty of people saw you come down this alley. If they were hunting for you, they would have searched this alley from top to bottom. These cellars would be the first place they would search. If you hide this gat, what can they do to you? Nothing. Nothing is what they can do to me. That teller did not see the gat in my pocket. All he saw was the bulge. He thought it was a gat, but he cannot prove it. You cannot send a guy up because you think he is packing a gat. You have got to see the gat. I did not say for him to fork over the money. I was too busy trying to get the gat out of my pocket to say anything. All I said was how much does it take to start a checking account? You cannot send a stiff up for asking about a checking account. No, even if they catch me, they can do nothing to me. But I will have to get rid of the gat. If they catch me with this gat on me, it will be just too bad.

I climb down off these rafters and stretch my legs. They are so stiff I can hardly move them. I hide this gat underneath a pile of rubbish in the corner. First I rub the finger-prints off. Me and this gat are finished. They can never prove that I owned this gat. I have got nothing to worry about. I

climb back up this coal-chute and into the alley.
I look around. There is no one here. They are not
hunting for me. I brush the cobwebs off me and
walk out to the street.

This guy in the tweed suit is standing on the
corner. I walk up to him.

"Buddy," I say, "I am down on my luck with no
place to flop. Could you spare me a few dimes to
get me a flop?"

CHAPTER SIX

I sit on this curb and watch these kids that stand in line. Their faces pale and pinched, tired and hungry. They wait, and fidget back and forth. Tin buckets, battered and rusty, are in their hands. They have had a lot of wear, these buckets. This is not the first time these kids have come after their suppers. One at a time they go into this mission. One at a time they come out with a bucket of soup and a stale loaf of bread.

This kid walks up to me.

"Mister," he says, "will you watch my bucket of soup and my loaf of bread while I go in and get some more?"

"Buddy," I say, "how much of this belly-wash

can you eat, that you want to go after two bucket-fuls?"

"One bucket is not enough," he says. "There are six of us. One bucket is not enough. They will only let you have one bucketful in this mission, so I leave one outside while I go in after the other."

"How do you keep them from knowing you?" I say. "Mission stiffs have sharp eyes. I do not see why mission stiffs don't get jobs as detectives, they have such sharp eyes."

"I am too smart for these guys," he says. "One time I wear this cap I have on. The next time I take it off. They do not know me."

"O.K.," I say. "I will watch your bucket."

He sets this bucket of belly-wash down at my feet and gets back in line.

I let my eyes wander over these women that stand in line. In a soup-line like this you will always see plenty of women. Their kids are too young to come after this slop, so they have to come themselves. I look at them. I look at their eyes. The eyes of these women you will see in a soup-line are something to look at. They are deep eyes. They are sunk in deep hollows. The hollows are rimmed with black. Their brows are wrinkled and lined from worry. They are stoop-shouldered and flat-chested. They have a look on their face. I have seen that look on the faces of dogs when they have been whipped with a stick. They hold babies in their arms, and the babies are crying. They are always crying. There are no pins sticking them. They cry because they are hungry. They clench their tiny fists. They pound them against their mothers' breasts. They are wasting their time. There is no supper here. Their mothers have no breasts. They are flat-chested. There is only a hollow sound as they pound. A woman cannot make milk out of slop. How much milk is there in a stale loaf of bread?

They shift their babies from hip to hip. They do not say anything. They do not talk. They do not even think. They only stand in line and wait. It does not matter how long. At first it matters, but after a while it does not matter. They are not going anywhere. When they have taken this stuff home and eaten it, they will be just as hungry as before. They know that. These babies will keep pounding their fists against their mothers' breasts. Tomorrow they will have the same hollow sound. They are all old, these women in the soup-lines. There are no young ones here. You do not stay young in a soup-line. You get crow's feet under your eyes. The gnawing pain in the pit of your belly dries you up. There are no smart ones in this line. The smart ones are not in any soup-line. A good-looking girl can make herself a feed and a flop if she works the streets and knows how to play the coppers right. She don't mind sleeping with a copper once in a while for nothing if he will leave her alone the rest of the time.

It is getting dark, and still they stand here. Their hollow eyes and their crying babies get on a guy's nerves. When this kid comes out of the mission, I hit down the skid row towards Karl's room. I huddle in these shadows across the street and watch this light in the window. It is the landlady's light I am watching.

This Karl is a friend of mine I met in the park. He has a job carrying out the garbage in a restaurant. He makes two dollars a week. It is dirty work, but two dollars are two dollars. He pays one dollar a week for this room. On the other he eats. He does not have to worry about coppers grabbing him by the scruff of the neck. He can tell all coppers to go to hell. When it is too cold to sleep in the park, I sleep on the floor of his room.

This friend of mine, Karl, is a writer. He is always hungry. You cannot stuff yourself on a dollar a week. It is not his fault he is always hungry. It is that nobody buys the stuff he writes. He writes of starving babies, and men who tramp the streets in search of work. People do not like such things. For in Karl's stories you can hear the starved cries of babies. You can see the hungry look in men's eyes. Karl will always be hungry. He will always describe things so that you can see them as you read.

I see this light in the window go out. Now is my chance. I cross the street and tiptoe up the rickety stairs. I can judge these stairs pretty well in the dark. This is not the first time it has been too cold to sleep in the park and I have used the floor of Karl's room. On cold nights the fifth step will squeak. On other nights it is all right. The one next to the top will always squeak, warm or cold. I am very careful to skip this one. This landlady has sharp eyes, and ears that are even sharper. Karl says she has a heart like a thermometer. Each ten degrees means one day you are behind in your rent. He says he likes to keep three days behind, as she is then nice and cool.

I turn the knob to Karl's room and walk in. It is dangerous to knock. Last night she caught me right in the doorway. I do not want to freeze to death again tonight. This room is only a hole, but it has a roof over it. That is something. It is not so much the cold, as the wet of the dew that you mind in the park. There is no furniture but a narrow cot and a rickety table. Karl is bent over the table writing. His pale, lean face and his deep-set eyes show that he does not sell any of the stuff he writes. You can believe that this one lives on a dollar a week for food. He jumps up when he sees me. He eyes the sack I have in my hand and grins. He has not eaten today. I can tell. When you are on the fritz long, you can tell when a guy has not eaten.

"Toppin's?" he says.

"Toppin's," I say, "and more than toppin's. This is our lucky night."

He takes the sack out of my hand and looks in.

"Great God," he says, "a coconut pie! A real honest-to-God coconut pie!"

He pushes his papers to one side and spreads this stuff out on the table. We are both excited. Our eyes glisten. Our mouths water. Never have I seen a prettier sight than these doughnuts and rolls, and in the center, standing out proudly above all, this coconut pie. It makes a sight for sore eyes. Some of these rolls are filled with jelly. Some are covered with powdered sugar. But this coconut pie is the prize. It is two days old and squashed in the middle, but it is something to look forward to, squashed in the middle or not.

Karl fills the coffee-pot with water. I unscrew the mantle from the gas-jet. It is a small flame. It is a hard job to hold the pot over it. The handle gets red-hot. We take turns holding it. We are both sweating when it is done, but it is good coffee. I do not lose any time screwing the mantle back on. We must have light, and besides, if the landlady found out we were pulling this little trick on her, it would be just too bad for us.

"Werner?" says Karl.

"Why not?" I say. "I saw him on the street this morning. He had a look in his eyes like Jesus Christ. He gets that look when he has not eaten for three days."

Karl goes across the hall to get Werner. Werner is an acquaintance of ours. He is an artist. He paints pictures of people he sees in the park. All the people in his pictures have a hungry look in their eyes. He has no better luck selling his pictures than Karl does with his stories. They are good pictures. People will not buy them, though. I think it is because of the hungry look. Even the picture of the fat millionaire leading the Peke dog had a hungry look in the eyes. Karl says it is more than an empty belly that puts a hungry look in people's eyes. I think that if Werner would take the hungry look out of the eyes of the people in his pictures, he could buy more hamburger steaks and take the hungry look out of his own eyes. Karl and Werner say this would be sacrilege to art. I do not understand such talk as this.

Whenever Karl and me run into some extra money, we buy groceries with it. We keep them in a closet for a rainy day. For a while our groceries disappeared. Not much. Only a little. A can of beans, a loaf of bread, a few stale doughnuts. We locked the door when we would leave the room. It did no good. Any key will fit his door.

"We will have to do something," says Karl. "We can't always be staying in the room."

"Leave that to me," I say. "I know a little trick that will stop a guy from stealing another guy's beans."

I go to the drug store and buy me ten cents' worth of croton oil. We pour this into a bowl of beans and mix it well. We leave this bowl on the table and go down the street. We are gone ten minutes. We come back, and our bowl is there, but our beans are gone.

"Now what?" says Karl.

"The toilet, that's what," I say.

"What about the toilet?" he says.

"We watch the door," I say.

The toilet is across the hall. We can see it from our door. We open the door a tiny bit and watch through the crack. For a half-hour nothing happens. Then comes this commotion down the hall. Werner lives down the hall. We see him shoot out his door. He is headed for the toilet. He is not losing any time. We watch through the crack till he goes back to his room.

"Now for the fun," I say.

"Fun enough already," says Karl. He is doubled

up on the floor from laughing. "Did you see the look in his eyes when he turned the knob of the toilet door? 'Oh, God, don't let there be anyone in there,' they said."

"Wait," I say. "You have not seen half. Do you know what I am going to do?"

"No," he says, "what are you going to do?"

"We are going in the toilet and lock the door," I say. "He will be back. There was plenty of croton oil in those beans."

"But," says Karl, "if he can't get into the toilet he will— No," he says, "we can't do that. That is more than he deserves. He has suffered enough."

Karl is too soft-hearted, but we have fun enough through the crack in the door. Three more times Werner dashes through the hall. Each time we roll on the floor and laugh till the tears roll down our face. After that there is no more stealing. We can now put anything in the closet. It is not bothered. But when we run into an extra treat like this coco-nut pie, we invite Werner.

Karl comes through the door. Close behind him is Werner, with his pale face, and his coal-black eyes in hollow sockets. Tonight he looks even hun-grier than ever. His eyes pop when he sees what is on the table. He licks his lips. We should not have put all this stuff on the table at once. A shock like this is not good for him. It might kill him. Werner's masterpiece will never be such a picture as this.

There is but one cup for the coffee, but there is the bowl and the glass. I fill up the cup for Karl. I take the bowl. Werner must take the glass. Karl sits on one edge of the bed. Werner sits on the other. I squat cross-legged on the floor. It would be more comfortable in Werner's place on the bed, but I am making up for giving him the glass. First we pass the doughnuts. One to each. When we finish this one, we pass them again. Each time Werner is finished long before us. He waits until we are finished. He licks his lips and glues his eyes to the table, then shifts them to the only thing on the wall, this sign which says: "Anyone stealing blankets from this room will be prosecuted."

"Who gave you these?" says Karl; "the baker?"

"The baker's daughter," I say.

"Is she beautiful?" he says. "She must be beautiful. None but beautiful women should touch such toppin's as these."

"She is so-so," I say. "Very pretty; but beautiful —I would not say that."

"Marry her," says Karl. "Marry her and bring her and her beautiful toppin's to live here."

"You never can tell," I say.

"How would you like that?" Karl says to Werner. "A beautiful baker's daughter to furnish inspiration to your art, and toppin's to put meat on your skinny shanks?"

Werner does not answer. He keeps his eyes glued to the doughnuts on the table. Before we are too full, we cut the pie. We still want to be hungry when we eat this pie, because it is a treat. Not often do we run into such a treat as a coconut pie.

That was a good guy, that baker. His heart is in the right place. He is not a beautiful girl like I tell Karl and Werner. He has a straggly mustache and wheezes through his nose when he breathes. If he has a beautiful daughter, I do not know about her. I only say she gave me this stuff in order to show off a little bit in front of Karl and Werner.

We finish this stuff and loosen our belts. We are filled to the brim. Already the haunted look is gone from Werner's eyes. He has even smiled a couple of times between mouthfuls.

"Some day there will be an end to all this," says Karl. "Some day we shall have all we want to eat. There is plenty for all. Some day we shall have it."

"Revolution?" says Werner.

It is the first word he has spoken since he came into the room.

"Revolution," says Karl. "Not now. There is no leader. But some day there will arise a leader for the masses."

"You are right," says Werner. "Some day there will be plenty for all."

He looks at these crumbs still left from the doughnuts on the table, and his eyes light up. If I was a capitalist, I would steer clear of Werner when the day arrives.

I am tired of such talk as this. You can stop a revolution of stiffs with a sack of toppin's. I have seen one bull kick a hundred stiffs off a drag. When a stiff's gut is empty, he hasn't got the guts to start anything. When his gut is full, he just doesn't see any use in raising hell. What does a stiff want to raise hell for when his belly is full?

"It is not right," says Karl. "There is no justice in this world. They do not know, they do not see what I see in the parks and in the soup-lines. Yesterday I sat in the park and watched these clouds that hung low and black in the sky. I like to sit and watch the stiffs that sprawl in the park. I watch them as they look at the clouds that roll through the blackening sky. They sniff the air. They can smell the storm. I watch them scurry to their holes like rats. I am lucky, I think, to have a hole. This woman on the bench beside me has no hole. The baby in her arms has no hole. I can tell. I can tell by the way she glances at the sky above, and the way she frets with the blanket on the baby as she hears the thunder roar. She is a young woman, a young woman who has forgotten what a hamburger steak looks like. I can tell by the look in her eyes. A hungry look. A look like Werner gets, and you and me. A look like Jesus Christ around the eyes.

" 'You had better hit it for cover,' I say to her. 'This is going to be a real storm.'

"She stares at me as though she does not hear me.

" 'Storm?' she says. 'Oh, yes, storm.'

" 'The baby will get wet,' I say. 'The blanket is not much. You had better get in out of the rain.'

" 'No place to go,' she says.

" 'It is hell,' I say.

" 'Yes,' she says, 'for the baby. For me I don't mind. I'm used to the rain and the wet.'

" 'How old?' I say.

" 'Two weeks,' she says. 'Two weeks tomorrow.'

"Straight ahead she looks into the dark. I sit there and wonder what she is thinking. If I knew what she is thinking, I would not be living in a hole in the wall, I think. I would write the book that I will write some day when I find out what they are thinking when they sit in the parks and stare unseeing into the dark.

"This cop comes up the walk and looks at us sharp.

" 'Better get your wife and kid home, Jack,' he

says. 'Regular hurricane blowing up. Be here in ten minutes.'

" 'Yes, sir,' I say, 'yes, sir. She sure is blowing up.'

"I get up. The woman sits there staring. In my pocket I am holding twenty cents. I finger it.

" 'Lady,' I say, 'you can't sit here in the storm. The baby will die of the croup.' I hold out one of my ten-cent pieces to her. 'Go over to that coffee joint and wait till she's over. You can get yourself a good meal in there for a ten-cent piece.'

"She holds out her hand and takes the money. I can tell by the way she takes the money that I was right. She is starved.

" 'Thank you,' she says, 'oh, thank you.'

" 'That's all right,' I say.

"I hit up the street. I look back and see her hugging this baby to her and heading across the street to this coffee joint. I stay in this pool hall until the storm is over. When I come out, I go into this joint myself for my coffee. This woman is still there. She sits by the window. I get my coffee and walk over to her table and sit down. She does not notice me. She keeps staring out of the window. Across the street that glistens with the rain, is the park. It is miserable over there now. Miserable and black and wet.

WAITING FOR NOTHING

" 'Well, I see you got in out of the wet all right,'
I say.

"She turns in her seat quick. She jumps when
she sees me.

" 'Oh,' she says, 'I—I thought you'd gone.'

" 'I came back for my coffee,' I say. 'You get
good coffee in here for a nickel. Up the street they
hold you up for a dime. A dime for a cup of coffee,
and lousy coffee to boot.'

" 'Yes, yes,' she says. 'Lousy coffee.'

"She keeps staring out of the window. There is
a wild look in her eyes.

" 'I got my opinion of a guy who will charge a
stiff a dime for a cup of lousy coffee,' I say.

" 'Yes,' she says. 'Yes. Lousy coffee. Lousy coffee.'

"I can see that she is talking batty. There is
something wrong. I thought that there was something wrong when I first sat down at this table. I
know what it is now. It is the baby. The baby is
not here. She has not got the baby.

" 'Where is the baby?' I say.

"She does not answer.

"I follow her stare out the window. Great Christ!
Through the blackness of the park I can see a
white splotch on one of the benches. I know what
that is. It is the baby. She has gone back after the
rain and put it there. She waits here to see if anybody picks it up. We do not say anything more for

106

a while. We just sit here and glue our eyes to this white splotch on the bench in the park.

" 'Can he roll off?' I whisper.

" 'He can't roll off,' she says. 'I pinned his blanket to the bench.'

"We watch this stiff come ambling up the walk of the park. He stops by the bench, peers down, and then hot-foots it across the street. He hurries back with this cop who stands on the corner. The cops looks at this white splotch on the bench and then walks back to the corner and makes a call from the box.

"This woman gets up. She has seen all she wants to see. She pulls her hat tight over her eyes. She does not want this cop to recognize her.

" 'Thanks for the money,' she says.

" 'That's all right,' I say.

" 'He was only two weeks old tomorrow. He will not miss me. Do you think he will miss me?'

" 'He is too young to miss you,' I say. 'They will take good care of him. You had better beat it.'

"She goes out the door and hurries down the walk.

"I sit there and sip my coffee. An automobile pulls up at the curb. The cop gets the baby and hands it to a woman in the back seat. When the car pulls out, this cop stands there and looks around the park. He is hunting for someone. He stops several stiffs that pass by. He talks to them awhile, and they go on.

"Christ Almighty! I happen to think. That cop is hunting for me. He thinks that is my kid. They would not believe me if I told them that was not my kid. They would put me in and throw the key away. I get up from the table and beat it outside. I stick close beneath the awnings and beat it home."

Karl stops talking. He thinks this is something new and something awful, this woman leaving her baby in the park because she cannot feed it. Karl is soft-hearted. That is nothing. I have seen worse than that. I know that that is nothing.

I walk to the window and look out. It has started to rain. It splashes and rattles against the panes. Below me the streets glisten and shine in the dark. A stiff slouches under an awning down there. He is soggy and miserable. He presses himself tight against the side of the building, but he cannot get away from the rain. You never can get away from the rain. I know. It is a miserable night, and he is miserable. I imagine him as he walks the streets in the rain. He passes houses and sees into the front windows from the street. He sees the people who live in these houses. They sit by their firesides. They are warm and dry. He is wet and cold. They are reading about him in their papers. They do not know it is about him, but it is.

WAITING FOR NOTHING

"I see by the papers," they say, "where they are starting a new soup-line on Tenth Street. Things are tough. Too bad things are so tough."

They turn over to the next page. The stiff in the rain is forgotten. But the stiff in the rain cannot forget. The water trickling down his soggy clothes will not let him forget. The gnawing pain in the pit of his belly will not let him forget. There are many funny things happen in the park, and on the street, too.

I stretch out on the floor by the window and close my eyes.

CHAPTER SEVEN

IT SNOWS. It melts as it hits, and the slush is inches thick on the pavement. The soles of my shoes are loose. The right one flops up and down as I walk. This morning I tied it to the toe of my shoe with a string, but the string wore through in an hour. Tomorrow I will tie it up with a piece of wire. It will stay a week if I tie it up with a piece of wire. My shoes are filled with water. I can feel it oozing through my toes as I walk. I walk and I can see the bubbles slosh from the soles. I am chilled to the bone. I pull my coat collar up around my ears, but it does no good. The chill comes from my soggy feet and the wind that howls round the corners. Besides, my coat is thin. I bummed it from an undertaker. The stiff that owned it croaked in the park with T.B. There's still a smudge of blood on the sleeve from the hemorrhage. I could have had his pants and shoes, too, but they were worse than mine. This coat is my Christmas present. For this is Christmas Eve.

There are lights in all the stores. They are packed with people, buying. A big arch stretches across the street. It is decorated with gold and silver tinsel. Across it, in different colored lights, it says: "Merry Christmas." The streets are choked with people. They crowd and shove. Everybody is laughing. I wonder how it feels to laugh like that? That fellow and his girl in front of me have been laughing for a block. He has bundles piled clear to his chin. When one starts to slip, she gives it a poke back in place, and they both laugh. They do not laugh because she pokes the bundles back in place. They laugh because they are crazy about each other. Besides, it is Christmas Eve. He is sporting a fur overcoat, and his shoes do not slosh when he walks. It is easier to laugh when you are warm and your shoes do not slosh.

Across the street is a restaurant. The electric sign over the door blinks on and off in the dark: "Eat— Eat—Eat." It looks warm in there. Warm and dry. Out here it is wet and cold. It would be nice to sit in there on Christmas Eve and watch how miserable it is outside. But that is not for me. I am holding a four-bit piece. A four-bit piece to celebrate Christmas Eve with. I stop and listen to this band that plays on the corner. They are playing Christmas music. I know the piece they are playing. It is "Silent Night." My mother used to sing me that song when I was a kid. That was a long time ago. Long before I went on the fritz. Here I am now with the sole of my right shoe flopping up and down. Here I am now huddled down in my ragged undertaker's coat.

I walk towards my flop on the skid road. I am hungry, but I cannot eat. If I eat, I cannot sleep. It is too cold to flop in the park in the snow. It is Christmas Eve and I am hungry.

I pass this dark doorway and see this girl who stands inside. She is on the make. I can tell by her look. She steps out of the shadows.

"You—you want to go with me?" she says.

I look at her in her cheap red dress and her blue tam. I look at the scared look in her eyes. She is not the type. I can tell. I have seen too many. She is nervous. She pulls at her handkerchief.

"Where are you going?" I say. I am only joking.

"I—you—you don't understand," she says.

She looks down at her feet. I notice that her shoes are worse than mine. The runs in her hose start at her shoes and go to the hem of her dress. I can see that she is the same as me.

"You are not used to this," I say. "You are not so good at it. Why don't you go to the mission?"

"I am not used to it at all," she says. "You are the first one. I guess I am sort of clumsy, but I'll learn."

"Not if I can help it," I say. "You hungry?"

"That's why I am on the street," she says. "I'm damn near starved."

"I am holding four bits," I say. "Let's eat."

"I should not be bumming meals off another stiff," she says, "but I'd cut your throat for a hamburger steak."

We walk down the street towards the restaurant on the corner.

"I've got an idea," she says. "Two meals in a restaurant will take all that money. Now, I've got a room with a hot plate in it. We will take this money and buy enough groceries for five or six meals."

"That is a good idea," I say. "I will do the buying. I am an old-timer. I know how to do this. I will go in the stores. You wait outside for me."

I go into this cigar store on the corner and change two of my ten-cent pieces for pennies. I am going to penny-up on these store guys. We pass this meat market. There are chickens strung across the window on strings. They look good. We lick our lips as we stand outside and watch them. They would go good doused in mud and baked over a jungle fire. But baked chickens are not for the likes of us. We are only a couple of hungry stiffs, and we are on the make for a beef stew. I walk into this joint. She walks up the street to the corner and waits.

This butcher is red-faced and fat. His belly hangs in folds over his belt. If I was holding what it took to put that belly on him, I would not have anything to worry about. He grins at me when he sees me. He thinks I am a cash customer. It is cash customers who buy the chickens that hang from strings in his window.

"Buddy," I say, "I am on the fritz and only holding three cents. Could you sell a guy three cents' worth of old baloney butts?"

The grin comes off his face. I knew it would. Nobody has any use for a stiff, not even a pot-bellied butcher. He scowls and reaches down in the box where he keeps his dog meat. He fishes out two baloney butts. They are green at the ends. Not for me, mister. I see a stiff almost die one night from eating green baloney butts. No, sir, there are too many baloney butts in this world for me to eat green ones.

"Jack," I say, "these baloney butts are green. I can't be paying good dough for green baloney butts."

"What do you want for three cents?" he says.

"I want some good baloney butts," I say. "Baloney butts that are not green at the edges."

"You are damn particular for a stiff," he says.

"It is my dough and my stomach," I say.

He cusses under his breath, but he digs up two baloney butts that are not green. I hand him my three cents and he takes it. The tight bastard. Soaking a stiff three cents for a couple of green baloney butts. I walk up to the corner and give this package to the girl. We walk on.

"We have got the meat," I say. "Pretty soon we will have the bread. I know how to do this."

We pass this bakery, and I go in. There is a woman behind the counter.

"Lady," I say, "I've only got two cents. Could you maybe sell me a stale loaf of bread for two cents?"

She hands me a stale loaf of bread. She does not reach out her hand for the two cents.

"Keep the two cents for the onion," she says. "You can't make a decent stew without an onion."

I can see that this woman is all right. I can see that she knows what it is to be hard up. She is not like that pot-bellied butcher. He is a bastard. I go outside and give this bread to the girl to carry. I do not want to be carrying anything when I go in the stores. It does not pay to look too prosperous when

115

you are pennying-up on the store guys. When we pass a place that looks good, I go in. Pretty soon we have all the stuff we can carry. My twenty cents are gone, but we still have thirty cents to use when this stuff is gone. You cannot beat pennying-up. Once in St. Louis I ate for a week on three cents. I made the restaurants.

"Could you maybe give a hungry stiff a half a cup of coffee for three cents?" I would ask them.

I am not begging anything. If a whole cup of coffee costs five cents, a half a cup will only cost two and a half cents. I am giving them a chance to make a half a cent on me. But they do not give me a half a cup. They give me a whole cup, and something to eat with it besides. I would be eating yet on that three cents only some bastard like that pot-bellied butcher took my capital away from me. Some guy like that is always taking a stiff's capital away from him.

We walk towards her room.

"How long have you been doing this?" she says.

"So long I have forgotten how long," I say.

"Do you mind it very much?" she says. "Do you mind asking for two old baloney butts when there are people to hear you ask?"

"I used to mind," I say. "I used to live on dough-nuts and coffee because I was ashamed for people to hear me ask. But you can't live forever on coffee

116

and sinkers. You get all greasy inside. Some time
you have to get a square meal to hold your stomach
in shape. It will shrivel up on you on coffee and
sinkers."

"Does it take long to get used to it?" she says.
"Don't you always mind a little?"

"It is the bastardly butchers who take your pennies away from you and cuss you under their breath
that you mind," I say. "You don't mind the ones
like the woman in the bakery. She knows that times
are tough. She has been hard up herself. She will
help a hungry stiff with a stale loaf of bread."

"Why don't you hit the houses for something to
eat?" she says. "Won't they feed you at the houses?"

"I will always hit me a house if I can find me a
yellow house," I say. "I have good luck at a yellow
house, but not too yellow. Some stiffs will not hit
any but a green house, but give me a yellow every
time, but not too yellow. It must be just the right
shade of yellow."

"Do you ever hunt for a job?" she says. "Don't
you ever try to get off the bum and live decent
again?"

"Sure, sometimes I try," I say. "But what can a
stiff do? You ask for work and they laugh at you for
asking for work. There is no work. I hardly ever
ask for work any more. Sometimes as I sleep in the
park at nights, I wake up. I light my pipe and look

at the stars in the sky above. 'I am a man,' I think; 'this is no way for a man to live. Tomorrow I will get me a job. I will keep on asking until they give me a job. I will make them give me a job.' I puff at my pipe through the night, and I can hardly wait for morning so that I can get me a job. When the morning comes, it is cold. I shiver on the street in my thin undertaker's coat. I go to the factories on my empty stomach, I go to the stores and the restaurants. 'Give me a job,' I say, 'any kind of a job. I will work for whatever you will give me. I will work for almost nothing.' They shake their heads; there are no jobs. Finally I can't ask at any more places. I am too hungry. A man hasn't even the guts to ask for a job when he is hungry. Besides, it is day. Things look different in the day than they do in the night. At night as you lie in the park and look at the stars, it is easy to find a job. In the day, in the heat and the glaring light of the sun, it is not easy. It is hard."

We are hitting the red-light district. Her room is here. The red-light district is the only place where you can get a room for a dollar a week. I look at her. She looks at me. We are two people in the world. We are the same. We know that we are the same. Our gnawing bellies and our sleepy eyes have brought us together. We do not say any more. We do not need to. I have these bundles piled up to my chin. She takes my arm, and we walk.

We turn into the doorway of this ramshackle red brick building and climb the stairs to the fourth floor. The rug in the hall is ragged and dirty. The people who live here do not live here for the scenery. They live here because they have no other place to live. The cops will not bother you for working the streets here. That is what these streets are for. We go into her room. It is only a two-by-four hole, but is clean. She keeps it that way herself. It has a bed and a chair. A hot plate sits on a box. You eat on the bed or the hot plate. It does not matter which so long as you have something to eat. I notice that the bed is a double bed. That is thoughtful of the landlady, because if the beds in the rooms were not double beds, there would be no use for the hot plate. There would be nothing to eat.

"This," she says, "is my boudoir and kitchenette. How do you like it?"

"It looks like a mansion to me," I say. "I have lived in the missions for two years."

I put the bundles down on the edge of the hot plate and sit down on the edge of the bed. I have walked the streets all day hitting the stem. I am tired. A four-bit piece is hard to ding.

She takes off her tam and starts to cook. I watch her as she cooks. She is pretty. Her hair, that is brown, and her eyes, that are blue, make her pretty. What she needs is a couple of square meals to fill up the drawnness of her cheeks and take the paleness from her skin. We talk as she cooks. I tell her about that bastardly butcher who took my capital away from me. She laughs. I laugh. We understand each other. We like each other. I am not like this because I want to be. She is not like this because she wants to be.

She peels the spuds. I clean the coffee-pot.

"James, the salt," she says.

"Yes, m'lord, and the pepper besides," I say.

We are having a good time. It does not take much for a couple of hungry stiffs to have a good time. The spuds that began to sizzle on the hot plate are enough. The pot of coffee that fills the room with its smell is enough.

"People meet in funny ways, don't they?" she says. "It was funny the way I met you, stopping you on the street."

"A stiff is always doing funny things," I say. "We can't act as other people act. We have got to do what we can. A woman turned me down for something to eat one time. I went out in front of her house and sat there on the curb all day with my head in my hands. In the evening she came out and gave me my supper. I worked in her garden for two weeks straight. I write to her yet sometimes. We have to act the best way we can."

"What did you think of me when I stopped you?" she says. "What do you think of a girl who will go as bad as that?"

"I think she was awful hungry for a hamburger steak," I say. "I think she has not had a hamburger steak for a week."

She laughs.

"And you are right," she says. "Not for more than a week. Two weeks. I had some turnips here and some beets. For three days I ate them. For two days there has been nothing."

"You look at things different when you have not eaten for two days," I say. "I know. I have gone that long myself. I have stolen. I have done worse than steal when I have gone that long."

"Yes, you look at things different," she says. "What is supposed to be wrong does not look wrong when the only right thing looks like something to eat. When I stepped out of the doorway to you, I wanted something to eat. Nothing was wrong that would give me something to eat."

"That is the way I felt when I started to knock a guy in the head once," I say. "That is the way I felt when I started to hold up a bank once."

"But you didn't knock a man in the head or hold up a bank?" she says. "You only started to. You didn't really do it?"

"No, I didn't do it," I say. "I only started to. I lost my nerve on the man. My gun got caught in the lining of my pocket, or I would have held up the bank. Maybe it is a good thing it did get caught. Maybe if it hadn't of got caught, I wouldn't be here. I am glad that I am here."

"I am glad that you are here," she says. "I am glad that I am here. I am glad that I stopped you on the street."

"I am glad you stopped me instead of someone else," I say. "Maybe this other guy would not know how to penny-up on the store guys."

"We will penny-up some more," she says, "but there must not be any baloney butts that are green at the edges. We can't be paying good dough for green baloney butts. There are too many baloney butts in this world for us to be eating green ones."

She is mocking me. We laugh.

"And the bread from the bakery," I say. "That bread was a little too stale. I am afraid that after this we will have to do our trading farther round the corner. For two cents we should get a fine loaf of rye bread that will be fresh, and not stale."

"We will trade at no place where they do not throw in some good cow's butter when you buy an onion for the stew," she says. "Cow's butter and cow's milk."

I walk to the window and look out. Through

the murk a million lights flash on and off through the haze of the snow. She comes to the window and stands beside me.

"On Christmas Eve a roof is something," she says. There are worse than us out there."

"Tomorrow where is the roof?" I say.

"Tomorrow is tomorrow," she says. "Tonight there is the roof."

I point to the rows of lights that span the bridge to the right of the town.

"There are a hundred stiffs live under that bridge," I say. "I have slept under there myself. I know. Men with wives. Men with children live under that bridge. That is their roof on Christmas Eve."

She takes my hand in hers.

"If you like, if you love the person you are under the bridge with," she says, "the bridge would not be bad. Even on Christmas Eve it would not be bad."

We stand hand in hand by the window.

"I like you," she says. "My name is Yvonne."

We laugh.

"My name is Tom," I say.

"Where are you staying at nights?" she says.

"In the park," I say.

"You can stay here," she says, "until the landlady kicks us out."

CHAPTER EIGHT

I WAIT, and, Christ, but the hour goes slow. I stand in this soup-line. Back of me and before me stretch men. Hundreds of men. I huddle in the middle of the line. For two hours I have stood here. It is night, and ten minutes before they start to feed. The wind whistles round the corners and cuts me like a knife. I have only been here for two hours. Some of these stiffs have been here for four. Across the street people line the curb. They are watching us. We are a good show to them. A soup-line two blocks long is something to watch. These guys on the curb are not in any soup-line. They have good jobs. They have nothing to worry about. It must be pretty soft not to have anything to worry about.

124

WAITING FOR NOTHING

Sixty seconds in a minute, I think, and ten minutes. That makes six hundred seconds. If I count up to six hundred, slow, they will be started when I finish. I began to count. I count to a hundred, but I can get no further. I have to stop. I am too cold to count. I stomp my feet on the concrete walk. I swing my arms high over my head. It is a damn shame to stand in this line as cold as I am, but I have to stay. I am hungry. I have to get a little something in my belly. I wait. We stiffs in the soup-lines are always waiting. Waiting for the line to start moving. The bastards. They keep us standing out in the cold for advertisement. If they let us in and fed us, where would the advertisement be? There wouldn't be any. They know that. So they keep us out in the cold so these people on the curb can have their show.

There is a commotion up in front of me. Stiffs bunch around in a knot. A cop pushes them back in line. There is a stiff stretched out on the ground. He is an old stiff with gray hair. His eyes are wide open, but he does not move a lick. He is tired of waiting for this line to start moving. He is stretched out on the concrete, and dead as four o'clock. I can see that this stiff is lucky. There will be no more waiting for him. They cover him up with a sheet and load him in the mission truck. He is off to the morgue. There is no fuss when a stiff kicks off in a soup-line. There is no bother. They throw a sheet over him and haul him away. All he needs now is a hearse and six feet of ground, and they will have to give him that. That is one thing they will have to give him. And it will not make any difference to him how long he has to wait for it. It must burn them up plenty to have to give a stiff six feet of ground for nothing.

This old stiff croaking like this out in the cold puts this bunch in a bad humor. They shove and cuss at these guys in the mission who make us stand in the cold. They can see that we mean business. They open the doors and let us in. A mission stiff hands us a pie pan, a tin cup, and a spoon. We carry them up to where these guys are standing over these tubs of stew. It is scorching hot in here. These mission stiffs that are ladling out the stew are sweating. The sweat drips from their faces and falls in the stew. But that is nothing. What is a little sweat to a stiff? What can a stiff do about it if it maybe turns his stomach?

We get our pan of stew and our cup of water and sit down at the table. The room is filled with these tables. A mission stiff walks along the aisles with a basketful of stale bread. He throws it to us like a guy throwing slop to hogs, and we catch it. This stew is made of carrots that were rotten when they were cooked, but we eat it. We have to. A stiff can't stand the cold outside unless he has a little something in his belly. I bolt down this stew and get out. The smell of this place will turn a guy's stomach. It smells like a slop-jar.

Now for a smoke. I am dying for a smoke, but I am not holding any smoking. I keep my eye peeled over the curb. A guy will throw a snipe on the walk, and a wind will come along and blow it over the curb. You will find your biggest snipes over the curb. I spot one in front of this drug store. It is a big one. It is not half smoked. I can see that the guy who threw this butt away was in the big dough. I slouch up to this snipe and stop. I put my feet between it and the store. I lean down to tie my shoe. I am not tying my shoe. I am picking up this snipe. What these guys in the drug store don't know won't hurt them.

I walk back to this mission and stop by this stiff who leans up against the telephone pole. He is sporting a pretty good front. He carries a roll of chicken wire under his arm. You can hardly tell this guy is a stiff.

"That was awful stew," I say.

"What was?" he says.

"That slop they feed you in the mission."

"You eat that slop?"

"What else is a guy going to eat?" I say. "A guy can't starve."

"A stiff with brains don't need to eat slop, and he don't need to starve," this guy says.

"Sez you," I say.

"Sez me," he says. "I have got a ten-cent piece." He pulls this ten-cent piece out of his pocket. "What would you buy if you had a ten-cent piece?"

I think. What can a stiff buy with a ten-cent piece when he is half starved? Well, a good cup of coffee will hit the spot right now. A good cup of warm coffee will go a long way when you are hungry.

"Coffee and sinkers is what I would buy if I had a ten-cent piece," I say.

"And that is just why you have to eat slop," he says.

"What has that got to do with me eating slop?" I say.

"You do not use your brains," he says. "Why do you think I lug a roll of chicken wire under my arm?"

"I have been wondering about that ever since I see you on the corner," I say. "Why do you lug it?"

"The coppers," he says, "that's why."

"What do coppers have to do with chicken wire?" I say.

"When you walk up the main stem," he says, "how do you go, fast or slow?"

"Any stiff knows that," I say. "I go as fast as hell.

If you do not go fast, the goddam coppers will stop you and frisk you on the street."

"You are right," he says. "But I don't walk fast on the main stem or anywhere else, and the coppers don't bother me."

"They don't bother you?" I say.

"They do not," he says. "They don't think I am a stiff. What would a stiff be doin' with a roll of chicken wire under his arm?"

"You are a smart stiff," I say. "I have never tried that."

"It's just as easy to be a smart stiff as a dumb stiff," he says. "All coppers are dumb. A smart stiff will fool a copper every time."

"You didn't say what you were going to do with your ten-cent piece," I say.

"I will show you some brains that are real brains and not imitations," he says. "We blow this dough for two doughnuts, see? Then we hot-foot it to a corner where a bunch of dames is waitin' for a street-car. We plant one of these doughnuts on the curb and go across the street. When enough dames is waitin' there, I duck across the street, dive at this sinker, and down it like I ain't et for a week. Dames is soft, see. This racket is good for a buck and sometimes two bucks."

I can see that this stiff has got brains, and what is more, he has got imagination.

"How long have you been working this little trick?" I say.

"Since I have been on the fritz," he says.

"And the bulls, don't the bulls ever break up your racket?" I say.

"Bulls!" he says. "I am too smart for the bulls. Come on, and I will show you why I don't eat the slop they throw out in the mission."

We go into this bakery and buy two doughnuts. They are no ordinary doughnuts. They are big and honey-dipped. I have never seen a prettier picture than these two doughnuts. That is because I am damn near starved. I want to sink my teeth into one of them, but I know that that is foolishness. After I was through eating it, I would be hungrier than ever. When you are starved and get a little something to eat, you are hungrier than ever. We can't waste any time eating one of these doughnuts. We are on our way to try out a little scheme that took lots of brains to think up.

We slouch down the street until we spot a good corner. There are a bunch of women waiting there for a street-car. When it comes along and they get on, we take this chance to lay one of our doughnuts on the curb. We put it in plain sight. Anyone waiting for a car can see it. I carry the other one, and we walk across the street and wait. In a little while there is another bunch of women on this corner.

WAITING FOR NOTHING

There are some men too, but we are not interested
in the men. Men are hard, but women are soft. A
woman does not like to see a hungry stiff starve to
death. A man does not care if a stiff starves to death
or not.

"Now is my chance," this stiff says.

He slouches across the street. I stand here and
watch him. He has got the guts, all right. There is
no doubt that this guy has got the guts. I can see
now why this guy does not need to eat mission slop.
A stiff with this much guts can live like a king. He
stops across the street and lets his eyes fall on this
doughnut on the curb. It is a picture sitting there.
I expect to see him make a dive for it, but he does
not. This stiff is deeper than that. He knows how to
do it. He just stands there and watches it. These
women see him looking. I can see they are thinking
why will a guy stand on the street and watch a
doughnut? He walks on by and stops a little ways
up the street. Pretty soon he comes back. He walks
far over to the curb and snatches it up on the fly.
He hits it over behind a telephone pole. By the
way he acts, you would think this was the first
doughnut this stiff ever snatched off the curb. You
would not think this guy has been pulling this gag
for years. He downs this doughnut almost whole.
It looks as though this stiff is plenty starved. You
would think he has not eaten in a month of Sun-

days. That is what these women think. That is what he wants them to think.

This big fat woman in the brown coat reaches down in her pocketbook and fishes out some change. She walks over behind the post and hands it to this stiff. He shakes his head no, but he holds out his hand yes. This guy wants it to look as though it hurts his pride to take dough from this woman. I can see that this guy will never need to swill slop in a mission. If one person is going to be big-hearted, everybody wants to be big-hearted. Four or five of these women fish around in their pocketbooks and walk over to this stiff who hides behind the post. This is real money. This is not chicken-feed that this guy is taking in. One of these women shells out a buck. I can see the green of it from across the street. If I had the guts, I can see that there would be one more dummy-chucker in this town tomorrow than there is today. You just dive down on a doughnut, and these women do the rest.

He thanks these women and walks up the street. In a little while I walk after him. I do not want these women to think I am with him.

"You are the stuff," I say. "That is the prettiest little trick I have seen in a long time."

"You will go a long way before you find a prettier little racket than dummy-chucking," he says.

"How much do you think I cleaned up on that doughnut?"

"I don't know," I say, "but I saw you get a buck."

"Two bucks and sixty-five cents," he says. "That is how much I made on one doughnut, and you wanted to spend that ten-cent piece on a cup of lousy coffee. You have got to have brains and imagination to get along on the fritz."

Me and this stiff hot-foot it to a restaurant and order up a good meal. This guy is all right. When he leaves he slips me a four-bit piece.

"Any stiff that eats mission slop ought to have his fanny kicked," he says. "There is too many doughnuts in this world for a stiff to eat mission slop."

I sit here in this restaurant and think. Why can't I do what this stiff does? I have as much brains as he has. I have the imagination, too. But I cannot do it. It is the guts. I do not have the guts to dive down on a doughnut in front of a bunch of women. There is no use talking. I will never have the guts to do that.

CHAPTER NINE

I CROUCH here in this doorway of the blind baggage. For five hours I have huddled here in the freezing cold. My feet dangle down beneath the car. The wind whistles underneath and swings them back and forth. The wheels sing over the rails. Up in front of me the engine roars through the blackness, that is blacker than the night. The smoke and the fire belch into the sky and scatter into scorching sparks that burn my back and neck. I do not feel the wind that swings my legs. They are frozen. I have no feeling in them. I slink far back in this door and put my hands over my face. Great God, but I am miserable. I cannot stand this much longer. I was a fool for nailing the blind baggage

of this passenger. I was a fool, and now I am freezing to death.

I think. How am I ever going to get off this drag
if it ever does stop? I can't walk. My feet, that
are frozen, will not hold me up. I sit here and
think, and I doze. I awake with a jerk.

"You damn fool," I say, "you can't go to sleep
here. You will fall under those wheels that sing
beneath you. Those wheels would make quick
work of you, all right. Those wheels would make
mincemeat of you. You would not be cold any
more."

I begin to sing. I sing loud. I yell at the top of
my voice, because of the roar of the wheels and the
sound of the wind underneath me. I don't want to
fall under those wheels. I am only a stiff, and I
know that a stiff is better off dead, but I don't want
to fall under those wheels. I can feel myself getting
dopey. I try to sing louder. I try to hear my voice
over the sound of the wind and the cars, but I cannot. I cannot keep awake. I can see that I cannot
keep awake. I am falling asleep. I wonder if this is
the way a guy freezes to death. I am not so cold now.
I am almost warm. The wind roars just as loud as
before. It must be just as cold as it was before. But
I am not cold. I am warm. Great Christ, I must
not let myself freeze to death. I swing my arms. I
reach my head far out over the side of the car. The

wind tears at my face, but I keep it there until the tears run down my cheeks. Oh, Christ, won't this drag never stop?

I feel the buckle of this drag beneath me. I feel it jerk and throw me forward. I hear the whine of air for brakes. I grab the sides of this car with all my might. My frozen fingers slip, then hold. I am not scared. I am not afraid. I just grab the sides of the car and hold. I feel this train slacken speed. I see the scattered lights of a town. Only a few lights, but I see that this drag is going to stop. I begin to laugh. I laugh like a crazy man when I see that this drag is going to stop.

I hang on with all my might. There will be a jerk when this drag stops. I do not want to go under those wheels. We pull to a stop in front of this jerkwater station. There will be no bulls in this place. The thing to do is to get off this drag before it starts again. It will not stay here long. How am I going to reach the ground? My legs are numb. They are frozen. They will not hold me up. I rub them fast and hard. I feel them sting and burn as the blood begins to run. I try to move them. I can move them. I can see them move. But I feel nothing when they move. I pull myself to my feet. I am standing. I can see that I am standing, but I cannot feel the car beneath my feet. I reach out over the side of this car and grab the ladder. I climb down.

WAITING FOR NOTHING

I hold with one hand and guide my legs with the other, but I climb down. I stop at this last step. It is a long way to the ground for my frozen feet. I jump. I fall face-down in the cinders at the side of the track. This drag whistles the high ball. She pulls out. I lie here in the cinders with my bleeding face and watch the coaches go by. I lie here in the cinders with my frozen legs that have no feeling in them. I shiver as I think of that blind baggage with the roar of the wheels and the sound of the wind underneath. I push my fists into the ground and get to my feet. I grimace at the pain that shoots through my legs, but I grit my teeth and walk.

What I want right now is a cup of coffee. A cup of good hot coffee will always warm a guy up. I am too cold to want to eat. I make it to the main stem of this town. There are lights in the few stores that are still open. I pass a restaurant. There is a sign in the window. It says: "Try our ten-cent hamburgers." I wonder if they would let a frozen stiff try their ten-cent hamburgers. I walk in. There are two customers eating. I walk up to this bird behind the counter. He backs away. He glances at his cash register. He has a scared look on his face. I look in the mirror that lines the wall. I do not blame this guy for being scared. What I see scares me, too. My face is as black as the ace of spades. It is smeared with blood from the cuts of the cinders

137

as they scraped my face. I hit those cinders hard.

"Buddy," I say, "I am broke. Could you spare me a cup of coffee?"

"I can't spare you nothin'," he says. "Beat it before I throw you out."

Imagine this bastard. I am half starved and half froze, and he turns me down for a lousy cup of coffee. I am too cold to even cuss him out. I want to cuss him out, but I am too cold. I walk down the street and hit these other two restaurants. They turn me down flat. I can't get me anything to warm me up. But there is one thing I will have to get, and that is a flop. In weather like this a stiff has got to have a flop.

"Where is the town bull?" I say to this guy on the corner.

"You will find him in the garage," he says. "He will be shootin' the bull by the stove in the garage."

I walk over to this garage and find this hick cop by the stove in the office.

"Chief," I say, "I want to get locked up in the can. I am on the fritz with no place to flop."

"The jail ain't no hotel," he says. "I can't lock you up. I can't louse the jail up by locking you up."

Well, if this is not a hell of a note! A stiff can't even break into a lousy can. They call this a free country, and a stiff can't even break into jail to get away from the cold and the wind.

"Can I warm up a little by your fire?" I say. "I am froze."

"Get this straight," this bull says; "we have no use for lousy stiffs in this town. The best thing you can do is to hit the highway away from here."

"What is a stiff supposed to do, shoot himself?" I say.

"If I catch you in this town tomorrow, it will be a good thing if you do shoot yourself," he says.

I go out to the street and walk. I walk fast. I do not feel like walking fast, but I have to to keep from freezing to death. That's how cold I am. I pass a pecan grove. Over away from the road I can see a shack with a light in it. I knock on the door. An old man comes to the door with a lantern in his hand.

"Hello," I say. "Have you got somewhere a guy could flop for the night around here? I am freezing to death, with no place to flop."

He puts his hand on the top of my head.

"Son, do you believe in Christ?" he says.

"Sure," I say, "I believe in Christ. Have you got some place I could flop around here?"

"The last days are upon us," he says. "The sound of the trumpet is soon upon us. Repent or you burn in everlasting flame."

This guy is as batty as a loon. I can see that.

"Have you got some place I could flop outside?"

I say. "An old shed or something?"

Outside will not be too far away from this guy. He is ready for the booby-hatch.

"The lamb that is lost is the care of the Lord," he says.

He leads the way to this building where they store the pecans. It is a big place. The floor is covered with piles of these pecans. He takes a shovel and digs a hole down in one of these piles. He puts two burlap sacks in the bottom of it.

"Son," he says, "lay down in this hole and rest."

I get in.

He covers me up with pecans, and piles sacks on top of me. My face is all that is sticking out of the hole. He puts a sack over my face.

"Rest that you may better fight the battles of the Lord," he says.

He takes his lantern and goes back to his shack.

It is pitch-dark in here now. I lie under these pecans and think. Here I am lying down in a hole. Here I am covered up with pecans. Before I went on the fritz, I was lying nights in a feather bed. I thought I was hard up then. I had a decent front. I had my three hots and a flop. Can you imagine a guy thinking he is hard up when he has his three hots and a flop? That was two years ago, but two years are ten years when you are on the fritz. I look ten years older now. I looked like a young punk

then. I was a young punk. I had some color in my
cheeks. I have hit the skids since then. This is as low
down as a guy can get, being down in a hole with
pecans on top of him for covers. If a guy had any
guts, he wouldn't put up with this. I think. Why
should one guy have a million dollars, and I am
down in a hole with pecans on top of me for covers?
Maybe that guy has brains. Maybe he works hard.
I don't know. What is that to me if he is there and
I am here? Religion, they say in the missions. Religion and morals. What are religion and morals
to me, if I am down in a hole with pecans on top of
me? Who is there to say that this world belongs to
certain guys? What right has one guy to say: This
much of the world is mine; you can't sleep here?

I lie here in the darkness and think. It is too
cold to sleep. On the blind baggage of the drag I
could not keep my eyes open. Now I cannot close
them. I listen to these rats that rustle across the
floor. I pull this sack off my face and strain my
eyes through the blackness. I am afraid of rats.
Once in a jungle I awoke with two on my face.
Since then I dream of rats that are as big as cats,
who sit on my face and gnaw at my nose and eyes.
I cannot see them. It is too dark. I cannot lie here
and wait with my heart thumping against my ribs
like this. I cannot lie here and listen to them patter
across the floor, and me not able to see them. I pull

myself out of these pecans and get to my feet. I tiptoe out to the road. I do not want to wake this crazy
old codger who dug the hole for me. I do not want
to hurt his feelings, and besides, he might go off his
nut.

I walk. I lower my head far down to keep the
whistling wind from cutting my face like a knife. I
listen to the creak of the trees as the wind tears
through them. I keep to the left of the road. I cannot hear the sounds of the cars as they come up
behind me. You can hear nothing for the roar of
the wind. From time to time I turn my head to
stare through the night for signs of a headlight.
When I see one, I stop in my tracks and hold out
my hand for a ride. They do not stop when they see
me raise my hand. They step on the gas and go
faster. They do not care to pick up a worn-out stiff
with blisters on his feet. It is night. They are afraid.
They are afraid of being knocked in the head. I
do not blame them for being afraid. You cannot
tell what a stiff might do when he is as cold and
fagged as I am. A stiff is not himself when he is as
cold as I am.

I reach the town and skirt it. I am afraid of rats,
and this town bull has a face like a rat. I reach the
yards and crawl into one of these cars that line the
tracks. I shove the door almost shut. I do not shut
it tight. If they start moving these cars during the

night, I want to be ready for a quick get-away. I take this newspaper out of my pocket and spread it on the floor. I take off my shoes and use them for a pillow. I lie down. I am all in. I am asleep in a minute.

I do not know how long I am asleep. I awake with a jerk. Something has awakened me. All at once I am wide-eyed and staring. There is a feeling of queerness in the top of my head. I know that feeling. I get that feeling when there is something wrong. I had that feeling once when a drag I was on went over the ditch. That feeling was in the top of my head just before a guy I was talking to on the street dropped dead. My breath comes in short gasps. There is a crawling feeling all over me. A tingle starts at my feet and runs to my hair. I feel a chill in the roots of my hair. I know what that is. My hair is standing up. I raise up on my elbow. The rustle I make as I move on the paper sounds like thunder in the quietness of the car. A ray of light comes through the opening in the door. It is not strong enough to reach to the other end of the car, but I know that there is nothing there. It is in back of me. Whatever it is that is in this car is in back of me.

I tell myself that there is nothing to be afraid of. There is nothing in this car but me, I tell myself. It is only a nightmare. You have ridden the blinds too long at a stretch. You are as nervous as a cat. You will have to take time out from the drags for a while and rest up in the jungles. You have been going at too steady a clip. But I only tell myself this to stop the tingle in the top of my head and the shivers that crawl up my back. Riding the drags does not do this to me. I have been doing it too long. I would not know what to do if I was not riding the drags. I know that there is something in this car. There is something near me. There is something in back of me. I can feel the eyes boring into the back of my head. When I feel like this I know that there is something wrong, something terribly wrong. Great Christ, but I am afraid. My flesh is goose-pimply. I want to scream at the top of my lungs. I want to make a wild dash for the door. I want to dash out into the night and run. I reach out and find my shoes in the dark. I put them on. I cannot tie them. My fingers tremble too much to tie them. I sit there and tremble and shake and try to get hold of myself.

"You are a fool," I tell myself, "a damn fool. The door is almost closed. You can't dash for that door. The thing that is in back of you would grab you before you could begin to get it open. Besides, who would want to hurt you? You are only a stiff. You are not holding any dough. What would anybody want to hurt you for? You must stay here. You

144

must stay here and wait."

For five, ten minutes I wait here, tensed on my elbow. Nothing happens. I feel the sweat pouring down my face. I feel it drip from my chin. It is cold in here, but the sweat drips down my face. I cannot stand this waiting in the dark. I will go crazy if I wait here any longer. I get to my hands and knees and start crawling towards the door. I crawl slow. Slower than I have ever crawled before. If you could see me, you would not think I was moving at all. Then I hear this sound. I stop in my tracks. It is only a little sound. A sound as though something were slipping up nearer and nearer. A sound as though someone was raising one foot and then putting it down. Then sliding the other foot up. Nearer and nearer.

Then, through the dark, comes this squeal. It is a wild squeal. A squeal like something is mad and crazy. It is like something that has lost its mind. I feel it bound through the air and land on my back. It knocks me down to the floor. These sharp claws bite into the nape of my neck. The long fingers grip my throat so that my breath comes in sobs. I am strangling. I grab at these claws. I feel a man's wrist. A strong wrist. A wrist that is all covered with hair like an animal's. I am down on my belly on the floor of the car. These fingers like hot iron press tighter and tighter. I feel these knees that bore

145

into the small of my back. My neck wrenches backward. So far back I wait to hear it snap. Dizzier I get, and dizzier. Like in a dream I know that these claws that bite into my neck are trying to kill me, to choke me to death. I struggle blindly in the darkness.

I throw myself to my back. I feel the claws loosen their grip. I feel them slide off my neck and tear the flesh off in strips. I feel the burn on my throat and the moistness that I know is blood. I stumble to my feet as he sprawls on the floor. I am facing him now in the dark. He scrambles to his feet. He is only a shapeless mass in front of me. It is a shapeless mass that wants to kill me, to choke me till there is no life in me. I see it hurl itself through the air. I brace myself against the side of the car and kick out with my foot with all my might. I feel it hit, hard. I hear a grunt, a squeally grunt that a pig might give. My foot is buried in his belly. He thuds to the floor. He rolls over and over, but he is up again in a second. There is a flash in his hand. Through the ray of light that comes through the door I see this flash. My spine creeps. I know what that flash is. It is a knife. I cannot let him get at me with the knife. I cannot let him rip me open with the knife. He is going to murder me with the knife. I have to get out of here. Great Christ, I have to get out of here. I leap towards the door and reach it. I claw

146

at it and try to pry it open. It is caught. The splinters bury themselves in my finger-nails. I do not notice the pain. I am too afraid to notice the pain of a splinter in my nails. Again behind me I hear that scream.

I swing around. The knife flashes through the air above my head. I grab at the hairy wrist that holds the knife. The razor-sharp edge slashes my arms. I know it slashes my arms because of the scorched feeling and the wet that spurts against my face. I struggle with the wrist that holds the knife and the arm that clubs at my head. I am getting weak. The loss of blood has made me weak. I cannot hold the arm that clutches the knife. I glue my eyes to this flash that quivers and shakes over my head as we strain in the ray that comes through the door from the moonlight. Nearer it comes and nearer. I twist the wrist with all my strength. I twist till I hear the snap of it through our panting and scuffling. I hear this scream again as the arm goes limp and the knife clatters to the box-car floor. I start to dive for the knife on the floor and feel this fist that smashes to my face. I sprawl to the other end of the car. I grope in the dark and try to get up. I cannot. I am too weak to get to my feet. I lie here and tremble on the floor.

Through the ray of light that comes from the door I see this guy stand and stare at the floor. The gleam of the knife is there. He does not pick it up. He is not looking at the knife. It is this pool of blood from my slashed-up arm he is staring at. He stares like a guy in a trance at this blood. He flops to his knees and splashes his hands in the blood and screams. He splashes his hands in the pool of blood and smears it all over his face. I can see him quiver and shake and hear his jabber as he smears the blood. I lie here and wait for the flash of the knife, but it does not come. He leaps to his feet and jumps towards the door of the car. He jabbers and babbles as he shoves against it. He slides it open and leaps to the tracks. I can hear his screams as he crashes through the thickets.

I lie in the darkness with my bloody arm and shiver and sob in my breath.

CHAPTER TEN

WE CRAWL on our hands and knees and ease up towards the yards. It is so dark you can hardly see your hand in front of you. We can hear them banging these cars around inside this high board fence that separates us from the yards. We can hear the switch engines chugging as they make up our drag. We do not have long to wait. We hear this drag give the high ball. We ease up as close as we can get without being seen by the bulls. We scrape our knees and our hands on the sharp pebbles in the tracks and stumble over the ties that are higher than the rest. We cuss under our breath. We crawl to the side of the tracks and press up tight against these piles of ties. We are nervous. A stiff is always nervous when he knows he has to nail a drag in the dark. This drag is pulling out. We see this shack on the tops wave his lantern to the engineer. We can hear her puffing as she comes. I cock my ear and listen to the puff. You can judge how fast a drag is coming by listening to the puff. This one is picking up fast. She will be balling the jack when she gets to where we are. I keep one eye peeled for the bulls. If they are riding this drag out, they will be laying for us. I have too many scars already from being sapped up by the bulls.

I can see her coming now. I can see the sparks that fly from her stacks, and the flames that leap above her. She is puffing plenty. She is a long drag, and a double-header. I can make out the sparks from the two engines. That is why she is balling the jack so much. This is a manifest. She won't lose any time going where she is going. Passenger trains will take a siding and let these red balls through.

This old stiff picks up his bindle, and starts back towards the jungle.

"This one is too hot," he says. "There will be another drag tomorrow. I do not like to sell pencils."

Four or five stiffs follow him. They know when a drag is too hot, too. They do not want to sell pencils, either.

WAITING FOR NOTHING

I crouch here in the dark and wait. Farther up the track I can see these other stiffs crouching beside the tracks. They are only a shadow through the dark. I hope I can make it, but I am plenty nervous. It is too dark to see the steps on the cars. I will have to feel for them. I pick me out an even place to run in. I look close to see that there are no switches to trip me up. If a guy was to trip over something when he was running after this drag, it would be just too bad. That guy would not have to worry about any more drags.

These engines bellow past us. I can see now that I have waited in the cold for nothing. I can see that a guy can't make this one. It is just too fast. The roar she makes as she crashes over the rails, and the sparks that shoot from her stacks, tell me she is just too fast. A stiff is foolish to even think about nailing this one. Christ, but I hate to wait all night for a drag and then miss it because it is too fast.

This stiff in front of me does not think this drag is too fast.

"Brother," I think, "I hope you are right, because if you are wrong you will not do any more thinking."

I see him run along by this drag. I see him make a dive at this step. He makes it. It swings him hard against the side of the car. I can hear the slam of his hitting from where I am. He does not let go.

151

He hangs on. I see him begin to climb the steps to the tops. Damn, but that was pretty. No waiting all night for a drag and then missing it for this guy. He is an old-timer. I can tell by the way he nailed this drag that he is an old-timer.

Another stiff runs along by this drag. I can tell that he is scared. He reaches out his hand after this step as this drag flies by, and then he jerks it away. This stiff will never make it. I can tell. He has not got the guts. A stiff has got to make up his mind to dive for those steps and then dive. This stiff makes up his mind to take a chance. He reaches out and nails this step. The jerk swings him around and slams him against the car. He hits hard. If he can hold on, he is all right, but he cannot hold on. He lets loose and flies head-first into the ditch at the side of the track. The bottom of that ditch is cinders. Christ, but there's a stiff that's dead or skinned alive. I cannot tell if he is moving in the ditch or not. It is too dark to see. I cannot go over there and see. I have waited all night in the cold to make this drag, and I am going to make it. That first stiff made it. If he can make it, I can make it. I have nailed as many drags as the next stiff.

"Be sure and nail the front end of the car," I tell myself. "Be sure and nail the step on the front end of the car. If you lose your hold, you will land in the ditch like that other stiff. That will be bad enough, but if you nail the rear end and lose your grip, you will land between the cars."

It is just too bad for a guy when he goes between the cars. I saw a stiff once after they pulled him out from under a box car. That stiff did not need to worry about nailing any more red balls at night.

I judge my distance. I start running along this track. I hold my hands up to the sides of these cars. They brush my fingers as they fly by. I feel this step hit my fingers, and dive. Christ, but I am lucky. My fingers get hold of it. I grab it as tight as I can. I know what is coming. I slam against the side of the car. I think my arms will be jerked out of their sockets. My ribs feel like they are smashed, they ache so much. I hang on. I made it. I am bruised and sore, but I made it. I climb to the tops. The wind rushes by and cools the sweat on my face. I cannot believe I made this drag, she is high-balling it down the tracks so fast. I am shaking all over. My hands tremble like a leaf. My heart pounds against my ribs. I always get nervous like this when I have nailed a drag at night going as fast as this one is.

I lie up here on the tops in the rush of the wind and wonder about that poor bastard over in the ditch. I wonder if he was killed. I know that these other stiffs who missed the drag will see to him, but I cannot get my mind from him. A stiff like that has

153

no business on the road. That guy should be a mission stiff. He has not got the guts to nail a drag at night. He should stick to the day drags. A stiff can't expect to reach up there and grab hold of those steps. You have to feel them brush your fingers, and then dive for them. If you make it, you are lucky. If you don't make it, well, what the hell? What difference does it make if a stiff is dead? A stiff might just as well be dead as on the fritz. But just the same I am glad I am here on the tops and not smashed all to hell underneath those wheels that sing beneath me.

For two hours I lie up here before this drag pulls to a stop at a red block. I am as stiff as board from the rush of cold wind and the frost that covers the tops. I will have to find me an empty. It is just as cold in an empty as it is up here, but there is not the rush of the wind that cuts through you like a knife. I climb down to the ground and run along by the tracks until I hear the voices of stiffs in one of these cars. I shove the door open and climb in. There are about ten stiffs already in this car. They are walking back and forth and stomping their feet from the cold. It is miserable in this car, and they are miserable. I am miserable myself. But then, what the hell? A stiff is always miserable. If he was not miserable, he would not be a stiff.

Some of these stiffs lie on the floor with last Sunday's newspapers around them for covers. They are not so cold. You will find a worse blanket than last Sunday's newspaper. I have no newspaper. I sit down in this corner and shiver. My teeth click together. On all sides of me I can hear other stiffs' teeth clicking together. The click keeps time with the song of the wheels on the rails. I close my eyes and try to sleep. But all I can do is lie here and think. I think: Here I am. I am in a box car. I am heading west. Why am I heading west? Well, it is warmer out west. There will not be the snow and the rain. You will not have to be listening to your teeth clicking together every time you try to get a little sleep. It is too cold to lie here. I get up and go over where these other stiffs are.

We huddle in a bunch. There is a pile of tar paper on the floor. We tear this up into small pieces and light it. The flames flicker up and light up our faces, grimy and sunken. The black smoke roars up and fills the car. We crouch around this fire and choke for breath. We do not mind the smoke if we can get a little heat. We stomp on the floor with our numbed feet. We swing our hands back and forth. We are just a box-carful of frozen stiffs. We do not make a pretty picture with our red-rimmed eyes and our sunken cheeks. We do not care whether we make a pretty picture or not. What we want is to get warm. I take off my shoes.

I hold one of my numbed feet over the flames. I
cannot feel the flame that burns my feet, but I hold
it there until my sock is scorched and burning.
Then I change to the other foot. Back and forth,
back and forth.

We huddle here and hack and cough in the
smoke. We do not dare to open the door. It will
not do for the shacks to see the smoke pouring out
of this car. They would sick the bulls on us at the
next stop. These bulls would put you in and throw
the key away if they ever caught you building a
fire on a box-car floor. Pretty soon we are out of
tar paper. We get out our knives and start cutting
splinters from the beams of the car. The beams
are hard. It is a tough job to cut fast enough to keep
the fire going. It goes out.

I crawl back in my corner and wait for morning.
The desert! That is a good joke. The books say
the desert is scorching hot. I wonder did any of
these guys that write the books ever ride across it
at night in a corner of a box car? I lie here in my
corner and listen to these stiffs' teeth clicking together. Even above the roar of the wheels I can
hear them.

"Goddam it," says this stiff in the corner across
from me, "I 'am not goin' to stand for this much
longer. I will get my hands on a gat, that's what
I will do. I will show the bastards I am not goin'

to freeze to death in a box car."

He stomps his feet on the floor to get the blood to running.

"Up your fanny," says this stiff he is with. "I have heard that old bull for years. If you are a stiff, you will freeze in box cars and like it. That's where a stiff belongs, in the corner of a box car."

"If I ever get my fingers on a gat I will show the bastards where I belong," this stiff says. "It will be just too bad when I get my fingers on a gat."

"Yeah, I said that, too," this other stiff says. "But I have got my fingers on a gat, and what did I do with it? Nothin', that's what I did with it. Nothin'. A stiff hasn't got the guts to do anything but eat slop and freeze to death. That's all he's good for. That's why he is a stiff."

I lie here in my corner, and I know that that stiff is right. That is all that a stiff is good for. I had my fingers on a gat, too. What did I do with it? Just what he did. Nothing. I maybe could have been on easy street now if I had gone through with that bank job. I would have either been on easy street or been under six feet of ground. And what difference would it make if I was under six feet of ground? Is six feet of ground any worse than lying here with my teeth clicking together to the tune of the wheels that sing over the rails beneath me? There is nothing worse than this unless maybe

it is being down in a hole with pecans on top of
you for covers.

This drag pulls to a stop at this water tank. A
draft of wind hits me. I can hear the door slide
open. It would just be our luck to have some shack
kick us off in this God-forsaken place. But it is not
that. Two new stiffs are climbing into the car.
They carry big flashlights in their hands. I can see
from the flash of the lights as they flash them around
in the car that they are a couple of mean-looking
eggs. Their faces are covered with dirty whiskers.
They have not had a shave in a long time. They
are filthy. There is no sense in a stiff letting himself get this filthy. There is too much water in the
world. One of these stiffs has a black patch over
one eye. He is wearing an old raincoat. The other
one is wearing a ragged brown overcoat and a blue
toboggan.

This drag gives the high ball and pulls out. I
lie here and listen to her puff, and wonder how
many more miles.

"All you bastards get over in the other end of
the car, and make it snappy."

I raise up quick. These two stiffs that just got
on are standing there in the doorway facing us.
They are holding their gats in one hand, and their
flashlights in the other. They look plenty tough
standing there. These big, black gats look plenty

tough, too. One of these guys has got his gat pointed straight at me. This drag is jerking and swinging over the rails. That gat is liable to go off any minute. I do not lose any time getting to the other end of the car. I can see that these two mugs mean business. If they do not mean business, why have they got these gats? And why does this guy have to pick on me to point his gat at? Why don't he point it at one of these other stiffs? There are plenty of other stiffs in this car besides me. These other stiffs do not like the looks of these gats, either. They get to the end of the car as fast as I do.

We know what this is. We know what we are in for. These stiffs are a couple of hi-jackers. This is a hold-up. I have got my opinion of any stiff who will hold up another stiff and take his chicken-feed away from him. Any guy who will do that is a low-livered bastard. I do not say that out loud, though —not with those gats pointed at us like that.

"Hold up your hands," this guy in the blue toboggan says.

We do not lose any time holding up our hands.

"You with the red hair, come out here," says this other stiff. "Any of you other mugs try anything funny and we will drill you full of holes."

This red-headed guy walks out to the middle of the car. He is holding his hands high in the air. They are shaking plenty. He is scared, and I can't say that I blame him. I am plenty nervous myself. These two are the toughest-looking mugs I have seen in a long time. One of them frisks this red-headed guy while the other one keeps us covered with the gat and flashes his light upon us.

"Where do you keep your dough?" this guy that's doing the frisking snaps.

"In my pants pocket," this red-headed stiff says. "In my left pants pocket. I've only got some chicken-feed."

"I will soon see how much you got," this hi-jacker says. "If I catch you holding out on me, I'll beat the living hell out of you and throw you out on the desert for the buzzards."

I can see that this stiff who is doing the frisking knows his business. I can see that he is an old-timer at this little trick of robbing stiffs of their chicken-feed. He not only looks in your pockets. He looks in the sweat-band of your hat and feels in the lining of your clothes. He does not find anything but chicken-feed on this red-headed guy.

"Get back in the corner," he says, "and keep your hands in the air."

He starts on the next guy. In the lining of this stiff's coat, fastened with a safety pin, he finds five bucks. Can you imagine that? This stiff has got five bucks pinned to the lining of his coat, and he has been bumming smoking off the rest of these stiffs. A tight stiff like that deserves to lose his dough.

"You will lie to me, will you?" says this hi-jacker.

He slaps this stiff across the face with the butt of his gat and knocks him clear across the car. This stiff sprawls on the floor and does not get up.

"Any of you stiffs make a move, and I'll drill you," says this stiff who is covering us.

We do not make a move.

One at a time he goes through the rest of us. I am the last guy. It is my turn.

"All right, you," he says.

I walk out to the middle of the car and hold out my hands. He goes through me. Four bits is all I got in my pockets. He does not find anything in my clothes.

"Where are you hidin' your dough?" he says. "Come clean or you will get what that other stiff got."

"Four bits is all I am holding," I say. "You've already got all the dough I'm holding."

"All right, get back to your end of the car," he says.

I get back. I feel pretty good. This bastard doing the frisking is not so smart. I bet I am the only stiff in this whole car who is holding a cent now. I am too smart for this bastard. I got two bucks hid under that bandage on my arm. I got iodine smeared over the tape. It looks like I got a plenty sore arm. But there is nothing the matter with my arm. That is only a way I thought up out of my head to keep these hi-jackers from stealing my dough. This is not the first time I have run into hi-jackers since I have been on the fritz.

This drag pulls over to a siding and slows down. She is going to let a passenger through. These hi-jackers pull the door open. They know she is going to stop here. I bet they pull this little trick every night.

"Lay down on the floor with your heads to the wall," one of them snaps.

We lie down. This drag stops. We hear these guys pile out the door. We hear the door close and the lock snap. They have locked us in. All these stiffs in the car get up to their feet and start cussing these hi-jackers. All but me. I do not say anything. I have got me two bucks under that bandage, with iodine smeared on top of it.

CHAPTER ELEVEN

IT IS night, and we are in this jungle. This is our home tonight. Our home is a garbage heap. Around us are piles of tin cans and broken bottles. Between the piles are fires. A man and a woman huddle by the fire to our right. A baby gasps in the woman's arms. It has the croup. It coughs until it is black in the face. The woman is scared. She pounds it on the back. It catches its breath for a little while, but that is all. You cannot cure a baby of the croup by pounding it on the back with your hand.

The man walks back and forth between the piles of garbage. His shoulders are hunched. He clasps his hands behind him. Up and down he walks. Up

and down. He has a look on his face. I know that
look. I have had that look on my own face. You
can tell what a stiff is thinking when you see that
look on his face. He is thinking he wishes to Jesus
Christ he could get his hands on a gat. But he will
not get his hands on a gat. A gat costs money. He
has no money. He is a lousy stiff. He will never
have any money.

Where are they going? I do not know. They do
not know. He hunts for work, and he is a damn
fool. There is no work. He cannot leave his wife
and kids to starve to death alone, so he brings them
with him. Now he can watch them starve to death.
What can he do? Nothing but what he is doing.
If he hides out on a dark street and gives it to some
bastard on the head, they will put him in and
throw the keys away if they catch him. He knows
that. So he stays away from dark streets and cooks
up jungle slop for his wife and kid between the
piles of garbage.

I look around this jungle filled with fires. They
are a pitiful sight, these stiffs with their ragged
clothes and their sunken cheeks. They crouch
around their fires. They are cooking up. They
take their baloney butts out of their packs and put
them in their skillets to cook. They huddle around
their fires in the night. Tomorrow they will huddle
around their fires, and the next night, and the

next. It will not be here. The bulls will not let a stiff stay in one place long. But it will be the same. A garbage heap looks the same no matter where it is.

We are five men at this fire I am at. We take turns stumbling into the dark in search of wood. Wood is scarce. The stiffs keep a jungle cleaned of wood. I am groping my way through the dark in search of wood when I stumble into this barbed wire fence. My hands are scratched and torn from the barbs, but I do not mind. I do not mind because I can see that we are fixed for wood for the night. We will not have to leave our warm fire again to go chasing through the night after wood. A good barbed wire fence has poles to hold it up. A couple of good stout poles will burn a long time. What do I care if this is someone's fence? To hell with everybody! We are five men. We are cold. We must have a fire. It takes wood to make a fire. I take this piece of iron pipe and pry the staples loose.

This is good wood. It makes a good blaze. We do not have to huddle so close now. It is warm, too, except when the wind whistles hard against our backs. Then we shiver and turn our backs to the fire and watch these rats that scamper back and forth in the shadows. These are no ordinary rats. They are big rats. But I am too smart for these rats. I have me a big piece of canvas. This is not

165

to keep me warm. It is to keep these rats from bit-
ing a chunk out of my nose when I sleep. But it
does not keep out the sound and the feel of them
as they sprawl all over you. A good-sized rat tramps
hard. You can feel their weight as they press on
top of you. You can hear them sniffing as they try
to get in. But when I pull my canvas up around
my head, they cannot get into me.

"Sniff and crawl all you damn please," I say.
"You can't get into me."

When I look at these stiffs by the fire, I am looking at a graveyard. There is hardly room to move
between the tombstones. There are no epitaphs
carved in marble here. The tombstones are men.
The epitaphs are chiseled in sunken shadows on
their cheeks. These are dead men. They are ghosts
that walk the streets by day. They are ghosts sleeping with yesterday's newspapers thrown around
them for covers at night. I can see that these are
ghosts that groan and toss through the night. I
watch. From time to time a white splotch gets up
off the ground. He cannot rest for the rats and the
cold. This is a restless ghost. Or maybe it is the
gnawing pain in his belly that makes him restless
and sleepless. The ground is hard. Damp and hard.
There are many things will make a restless ghost
at night in a jungle. I am a restless ghost myself.

I look from face to face about our fire. We are

not strangers. The fire has brought us together. We do not ask questions about each other. There is nothing to ask. We are here. We are here because we have no other place to go. From hollow, dark-rimmed eyes they watch the fire. Their shoulders sag and stoop. Men come to look like this when night after night they hunt for twigs through the dark to throw on a jungle fire. This hunchbacked guy across from me squats on his legs and talks. His voice is flat and singsong.

"I hit this state in 1915 with a hundred bucks I made in the harvest in Kansas. I pulled off this drag and made for a saloon in town. It was cold riding those rails, and I needed a drink to warm me up. Before I knew it, I was drunk and nasty. This spick lunged up against me at the bar, and I pushed him away. I never liked a greaser, any-way. Before I knew it, we were going after each other with our knives. I jabbed him one in the ribs. He dropped his knife to the floor and yelled. He wasn't hurt bad. Just a jab, but it scared him. Someone grabbed me and pinned my arms from behind. I thought they were ganging me. I was big and strong then. My back was hunched, but strong. I pulled away and let this guy have it. I got him right through the heart. He sagged to the floor. His hands rubbed against my face as he fell. Not hard. Just light. Light and soft like a woman's or a ghost's. I dream about those hands rubbing against my face light and soft when I sleep. I didn't know this guy was a deputy until they locked me up in the jug.

"Well, I got twenty years. That is a long time. It is a lifetime. I wrote my mother I was going down on a construction job in Mexico. That's the last time they ever heard from me. I wanted them to think that I had died down there. Fifteen years in the big house is the stretch I did. It ruined me. It would have ruined anybody. I was like I am now when I got out. My blood is all turned to water. I can't stand the cold any more. My blood is all turned to water.

"I bummed around on the rattlers after I got out. A bindle stiff was all I was. That's all there was to do. I was an old man. Then I got this crazy notion to go home and see how things looked. I hopped myself a drag and headed east. Well, it was the same old town. You know the type. Hardly a new building put up in years. I didn't hang around town much. The first thing I did was to go out to the cemetery. I was hunting a grave. My mother's grave. I didn't hunt long until I found what I was looking for. I knew it would be there. Fifteen years is a long time. I had a sister in that town, and a brother, but I had seen all I came to see. I turned around and walked back to the tracks.

There was a west-bound due out of there at night.
I nailed it."

He finishes. We do not say anything. We just
sit here and stare into the fire. There are a lot of
things will put a guy on the fritz. One minute
you are sitting on top of the world, and the next
you are sitting around a jungle fire telling about it.
The rest of these guys could tell their stories too,
if they wanted to. They have stories to tell. But
they do not say anything. Some stiffs do not tell
their stories. They walk up and down the garbage
heaps at night with the look on their face.

We hear the sound of voices over at the other
side of the tracks. They are coming our way. We
raise our heads. More frozen stiffs hunting a warm
fire, we think. But there is no such luck for us.
Four men are hot-footing it over the tracks. They
swing blackjacks in their hands. From their hips
swing gats in holsters. It is the bulls. By God, a man
can't even crawl into a filthy garbage heap for the
bulls.

"Line up, you lousy bums," the leader says.

He swings his blackjack high. He is aching for
a chance to bring it down on some stiff's head.

We line up. There are twenty of us. We are
twenty, and they are four, but what can we do? We
kill one of these bastards, and we stretch. They
kill one of us, and they get a raise in pay. A stiff

169

hasn't got a chance. They know a stiff hasn't got a chance.

"Hold up your hands," this leader snaps.

We hold up our hands, and they go through our pockets. They do not find anything. It makes them sore.

"I have a good notion to knock every one of you sons of bitches in the head and leave you for the rats," this guy says. "You are nothin' but a bunch of sewer rats, anyway."

He glances around the jungle. He sees our suppers that cook on the fires. He walks from one fire to the other and kicks everything over on the ground. I want to pull this bastard's guts out with my bare hands. We are twenty hungry stiffs in a jungle. We had to work hard to get that grub. A stiff always has to work hard to rustle up his grub. It is almost ready to eat, and he kicks it over on the ground.

"Get out on the highway before we sap you up," this guy says.

"You are a bastard," says this guy with the wife and kid, "a no-good bastard."

This bull walks up to this stiff and brings his blackjack down on the top of his head. It makes a thudding sound when it lands. He topples to the ground. The blood spurts from the cut in his head. He gets to his feet and staggers around the fire.

This woman with the kid starts to cry. We close in towards these bulls. We fumble on the ground for sticks and rocks.

"Let's hang the sons of bitches," says this old stiff, "let's skin the bastards alive."

These bulls see that we mean business. They go for their gats in their holsters. They cover us.

"I will bore the first bastard that lays a hand on me," this leader says.

We stop crowding in. What can we do when they have us covered with these gats? There is nothing we can do.

"Hit it down the pike as fast as you can go, and don't come back," says this bull.

We head down the road. It is the cold night for us with our blistered feet and our empty bellies.

Five miles down this road there is a water tank. Sometimes the drags stop there for water. If we are lucky, we can nail a drag out of there tonight. We walk. We have covered a mile when the man and the woman with the kid drop out. It is a rough walk over the ties in the night, and they are tired and hungry. They flop down on the side of the road to sleep. We go on. We can hear the baby strangling for breath behind us. We can hear the woman slap it on the back.

We stumble over the ties. It is too dark to see them. We get over to the side of the tracks and

171

walk. The burrs come up through the soles of my shoes, but I go on. I cannot stop. If I stop, I will not be able to get started again. My feet will swell. I trudge on, and when I take a step it drives the sharp points of the burrs far into my feet. I straighten my pack over my back and limp. I look at the stars in the sky above, and I see no comfort there. I think of that poor bastard lying back there in the weeds with his wife and kid.

"Oh, God," I say, "if there is a God, why should these things be?"

We hobble for hours with our heavy packs before we reach the tank. We flop to the ground beneath it. We pull off our soleless shoes and rest our blistered feet. We lie here like men that are dead, and look at the sky overhead. We talk back and forth through the night. We talk and we do not care whether anyone is listening or not. We do not care. We have to talk. That is the only way we can get our thoughts out of our minds. This hunchback tell his troubles to the stiff in the ragged red sweater. This guy in the red sweater does not care about the troubles of this hunchback, but he sees in his troubles some of his own. So he listens. This hunchback is not talking for himself. He talks for all of us. Our troubles are the same.

"For three years," says this old stiff, "I have laid in the cold and the dark like this. Is this goin' to last forever? Ain't things never goin' to be different? How long is a guy supposed to put up with this?"

"You'll croak in a jungle, and I'll croak in a jungle," this hunchback says. "Times'll never get any better. They will get worse. I got a paper in my pocket." He taps the newspaper in his pocket. "There is an editorial in this paper. It says this depression is good for people's health. It says people eat too much, anyway. It says this depression is gettin' people back to God. Says it will teach them the true values of life."

"The bastards," says this stiff gnawing on the green baloney butt, "the lousy bastards. I can just see the guy that wrote that editorial. I can see his wife and kids, too. They set at their tables. A flunky in a uniform stands back of their chairs to hand them what they want at the table. They ride around all day in their Rolls-Royces. Will you ever see that guy in a soup-line? You will not. But the bastard will write this tripe for people to read. True values of life, by God! If this guy wants to get back to God so much, why don't he swap his Rolls-Royce for a rusty tin bucket and get in line? The bastard."

"He says you can live on nothin' but wheat," this hunchback says. "He says this depression is nothin' to get excited about. People will not starve.

There is plenty of wheat. If a guy says he is hungry, give him a bushel of wheat."

"Where is the wheat?" this old stiff says. "When I come through Kansas, they was burnin' the goddam stuff in the stoves because it was cheaper than coal. Out here they stand in line for hours for a stale loaf of bread. Where is the wheat, is what I want to know."

"Try and get it," this stiff says, "just try and get it. They will throw you in so fast your head will swim."

Far away we hear this drag whistle in the night. It is a lonesome and dreary moan. We put on our shoes and go out to the tracks and wait. We lie down on the tracks and place our ears to the rails. We can hear the purr that rumbles through them. We look at each other and shake our heads. Too fast. If she does not stop for water at this tank, she is too hot to catch on the fly. A stiff just can't nail this one on the fly. We are old-timers. We know by the sing in the rails when a drag is too hot. We go back to our bindles and sit down. If she does not stop, there will be another drag tomorrow. What is a day to us, or a month or a year? We are not going any place.

We see her belch round the bend. She is not going to stop here, that is sure.

"She is coming round the bend," this kid yells.

WAITING FOR NOTHING

"Ain't you stiffs goin' to nail her?"

We shake our heads. Too fast. We know. We can tell by the puff, and the sparks that fly from her stacks.

He hits it over to the tracks and waits. Is this damn punk going to try to nail this one? If he does, he is crazy. But what the hell? All punks are crazy. They make it harder for us old ones. This drag whistles. She is batting plenty. The engine and a dozen cars pass us before we know it. She can't waste any time slowing up for a bunch of stiffs. This kid stands there by the tracks and watches her whiz by. He is making up his mind whether to nail it or not. He is a damn fool to even think about nailing this one. I have seen too many guys with stumps for legs to even think about nailing this one. I can still walk. That is something.

I sit here on my bindle and watch him. He is only a shadow by the tracks. The cars whiz by. He runs along beside her. He makes a dive for this step, the rear step. What is this damn fool diving for the rear step for? Don't he know enough to nail the front end of a car? She swings him high, and in between the cars. He loses his grip. He smashes against the couplings. He screams. He is under. Oh, Jesus Christ, he is under! He is under those wheels. We run over. He lies there beside the tracks. He is cut to ribbons. Where his right arm and leg were, there are only two red gashes. The blood spurts out of the stumps. It oozes to the ground and makes a pool in the cinders.

We drag him over to the side. He is through. I can see that he is through. His eyes are half shut. They are dopey-looking. There is a grin on his face. It is a foolish, sheepish grin. No stiff likes to have a drag throw him. It hurts a stiff's pride to have a drag throw him. It hurts this kid's pride, too, so he has a sheepish grin on his face, and him with his two stumps oozing blood to the cinders.

I lean over him.

"Want a cigarette, buddy?" I say.

"Hello, there," he says. "Sure, I want a cigarette."

I put it between his teeth and light it.

"My arm feels funny," he says. "Kind of numb and tingly. That old drag was balling the jack. I must have bumped it pretty hard."

"You got a rough bump," I say, "but you will be all right in a minute. She was a hot one, all right."

"She was plenty hot, all right," he says. "I thought I was a goner when I slipped."

He does not know he is hurt. He cannot see his two stumps that are oozing blood on the cinders. I lean over so he cannot see. What is the use to let him know? He will be gone in a minute. There is nothing we can do. His troubles will soon be over.

WAITING FOR NOTHING

I watch him. I am sick all over. I am watching a kid die. It is hard enough to watch anybody die. I even hate to watch an old stiff die, even when I know he is better off dead. But a kid is different. You kind of expect a kid to live instead of die.

There is no color in his face now. All the color is on the ground mixed with the cinders. He closes his eyes. The cigarette drops out of his mouth. He quivers. Just a quiver like he is cold. That is all. He is gone. I unfold a newspaper and cover up his face.

We sit there in the dark and look at each other.

CHAPTER TWELVE

I AM in this mission. I lie up on top of this bunk.
It is a high bunk. It is a three-decker. If I should
turn over on my stomach in my sleep, I would fall
out and break my neck. This is a big room. There
are a thousand here besides myself. I lie up here
and listen to the snores of a thousand men. It is
not funny. I lie here and listen to them snore, and
I cannot sleep for thinking. I look at the rafters
overhead and the shadows that play across them. I
think of vultures hovering in the sky, waiting.
They dart across the rafters and onto the walls. I
see them swooping down on their prey that lie
sweating in the lice-filled bunks. Their prey is a

thousand men that lie and groan and toss. I lie here and listen to them groan and toss, and I try to figure it out.

"There is no God," I say. "If there is a God, why is such as this? What have these men done that they live like rats in a garbage heap? Why does He make them live like rats in a garbage heap?"

It is all dark in here. Dark save for the light and the shadows that come from the electric sign outside. It is a big sign. It hangs from wires in front of this mission. "Jesus Saves," it says. I can hear the shuffle of stiffs as they slouch in front of the door outside. They lean up against the sides and sprawl on the curb. They are waiting for nothing. There will be no flop in this joint for them tonight. They are too late. There are plenty of beds left in here, but they are too late. You have to come early and listen to the sermon if you want a flop in this joint. They are too late. I lie here and wonder since when did Jesus Christ start keeping office hours?

There are gas hounds out there, too. I can hear them. They snore and groan in the doorway. They do not care where they flop. They do not care if they flop at all. They do not have a care in the world. I do not blame these guys for being gas hounds. They do not know what it is to be hungry. They never have to eat. What's the use of blowing a good ten-cent piece on a feed? You can blow it on a can of heat and forget you are hungry. You can forget a lot of other things besides.

I turn my eyes to the stiff in the bunk next to mine. Through the shadows I can see him lying there. His face is pasty white. The bones almost stick out of his skin. All you can see is the whites of his eyes as he rolls them back and forth. They are big eyes. Big eyes set in a skull with only a little meat still left. And they are all white. That's what gives me the willies when he rolls them about like that. There is no color in them. They are all white. I turn my head away from him, but still I can hear him groan. It is a hollow groan. It comes from a hollow chest. I cannot keep my eyes away from him. I cannot help looking at him. His hands are like claws lying there on the dirty blankets. He does not breathe. He only rattles. Why don't some-one do something for this poor bastard? Do some-thing! That is a good joke. When he rattles to death on top of this lousy bunk, it will only be one less to swill down their lousy carrot slop. God damn them. Some day they will pay for this.

"For Christ sake, what is the matter with that stiff?" says this stiff in the next bunk.

"He is croaking up here in his lousy bunk, that's what's the matter with him," I say.

"Does he have to make that much racket to

180

croak?" he says. "I see plenty of stiffs croak, but I never see one make that much racket at it."

"I guess a stiff has got a right to make as much noise as he wants to when he is croaking," I say. "Why should he care if a bunch of stiffs get their sleep or not? Nobody is worrying their heads off about him."

"Give him a swig of heat or knock him in the head," this stiff says. "They are kickin' me out of this joint tomorrow. I got to get me some sleep so I can ride the rattlers. A guy can't be ridin' the rattlers if he needs sleep."

I lie up here and think. Here is a stiff who has lived his life, and now he is dying under these lousy blankets in a mission. Who is there to care whether he lives or dies? If all this stiff needed was a glass of water to save his life, he would croak anyway. Nobody in this mission would give him a drink of water. This stiff is dying, and this other stiff in the next bunk is raising hell because the rattles from his hollow chest keep him from sleeping. This stiff has not always been a stiff. Somewhere, some time, this stiff has had a home. Maybe he had a family. Where are they now? I do not know. The chances are he does not know himself. He is alone. The fritz has made him alone. He will die alone. He will die cooped up in a mission with a thousand stiffs who snore through the night, but he will die alone. The electric light outside will go on and off in the dark, "Jesus Saves," but that will not help this stiff. He will die alone.

I yell to this mission stiff who is the night man.

"What the hell are you yellin' about?" he says. "Don't you know you will wake these other stiffs up?"

"There is a man dying up here in this lousy bunk, and you ask me why am I yelling?" I say. "Are you going to let this poor bastard suffer all night?"

"What do you think I am goin' to do with him?" he says. "I am no wet-nurse for a bunch of lousy stiffs."

"You are a God-damn mission stiff," I say, "and mission stiffs are sons of bitches."

"You can't talk like that to me," he says. "I'll have you kicked out of the mission. Tomorrow I'll have you kicked out of the mission."

"You call an ambulance for this stiff," I say, "or I will call it myself, and beat the hell out of you besides."

"I will call the ambulance," he says, "but you will not be here tomorrow. I'll see that you are not here tomorrow."

He cusses and goes out to the office to call the ambulance.

Pretty soon the doctor is here. There are two

guys with him. They are dressed in white. They carry a stretcher between them. This croaker climbs up on this three-decker bunk and looks at this guy. He feels his pulse and times it with his watch. He sticks a thermometer in his mouth. When he pulls it out, he shakes his head. He pulls out a piece of paper and a pencil.

"What is your name?" he says to this guy.

This stiff does not answer. He cannot answer. This stiff will soon be finished. There will be no more mission swill for this stiff. He walls his eyes and gurgles in his throat. He moves his claw-like hands. He wants to talk, but can't.

"Where do you live?" this croaker says.

This stiff does not answer him. He cannot tell him, but I can tell him. He lives wherever he can find a hole to get in out of the rain. He lives wherever he can find a couple of burlap sacks to cover up his bones. He cannot tell him this, because he is dying. I have seen a lot of old stiffs die. I can tell. His bloodless lips pull back over his yellow teeth. It looks as though this stiff is grinning at this croaker who asks him where he lives. I shiver in my blankets. This stiff is a ghost. A ghost of skin and bones. A bloodless ghost. I try not to look at him. A dead man's grin is a terrible thing. A mocking, shivery thing.

This croaker climbs down off the bunk.

"This guy has not got a chance," he says. "I can't do anything for this guy. He is starved to death. He is skin and bones. He will be dead in an hour."

"What'll we do with him?" this mission stiff says.

This bastardly mission stiff does not want to be bothered with an old stiff who will be dead in an hour. He is afraid he might have to help carry him downstairs. All mission stiffs are the same. They are all bastards.

"Load him up," this croaker says to the guys with the stretcher; "we'll take him with us."

They load him on the stretcher and take him out. He does not move his face. Only the whites of his eyes show as he walls them around in his head. Only the sound of the rattle comes from his hollow chest.

There are not a thousand snores through the night now. There are none. These stiffs in the bunks raise up on their elbows and watch these two guys in white carry this stiff out. These stiffs know what they are watching. They are watching a funeral. This stiff is not dead yet, but they are watching a funeral. He will not come back. You will see them carry out plenty of stiffs in a mission on these stretchers. You will never see them again after they carry them out. We know that we are watching a funeral. When they carry you out of a mission, you are dead.

WAITING FOR NOTHING

They thump down the stairs with this stiff. I lie up here and listen to them thump. These other stiffs lie back in their bunks. Some of them pull the covers up tight around their chins. They are cold. It is not so cold in this room. They are not cold because they are cold, but because they are afraid. I know what they are thinking. They think that that stiff on the stretcher they hear thumping down the stairs is not the stiff that is on it, but themselves. They can see themselves lying on this stretcher. They see the whiteness of their eyes walling through the darkness of the night. They hear the rattle that comes from a hollow chest. That is the way they will land up. They know that that is the way. You cannot forever be eating slop and freezing to death at night. Some night you will not be able to get your breath for the rattle, and they will come and carry you out on a stretcher. There is no snoring now. We stare wide-eyed at the shadows that play across the ceiling. We watch the flickerings of the sign outside that says: "Jesus Saves."

Underneath me is this itch and crawl. I tell myself it is the stickiness of the dirty blankets. But it is not that. I know what it is. It is lice that itch and crawl beneath me. I lie here and feel them crawl. I do not scratch. It does no good to scratch. I lie here and grit my teeth until I can stand it no longer.

185

WAITING FOR NOTHING

I pull these blankets off me and strike a match. I cannot see them. They are too small to see. I brush these blankets off with my hands. I take these newspapers out of my pants pocket and spread them over the bed. I leave some of the paper hang over the sides. Maybe if they try to crawl out to the edge to get me, they will fall to the floor and break their necks. I lie back down and spread the rest of these papers over me.

It is better now. There is no itch to make me lie and grit my teeth. It is better to freeze to death than to be eaten alive by lice. The stiff under me snores again and scratches. The stiff under him snores and scratches. I lie here and try to think back. I try to think back over the years that I have lived. But I cannot think of years any more. I can think only of the drags I have rode, of the bulls that have sapped up on me, and the mission slop I have swilled. People I have known, I remember no more. They are gone. They are out of my life. I cannot remember them at all. Even my family, my mother, is dimmed by the strings of drags with their strings of cars that are always with me in my mind through the long, cold nights. Whatever is gone before is gone. I lie here and I think, and I know that whatever is before is the same as that which is gone. My life is spent before it is started. I peer into the blackness of the ceiling, and in its blackness I try to find the riddle of why I lie here on top of this three-decker bunk with the snores of a thousand men around me.

I look over at this stiff's empty bunk. Dead in an hour. I shiver. Great Christ, I think, is this the way I will go out, too? It is hard enough to pass out in a nice feather bed with all your family gathered around and crying. It is no snap to die like that. But this way. Lying up on top of a three-decker bunk. No mattress under you. Only a dirty blanket. Lie here and rattle and groan. Lie here and feel the lice crawling all over you and under you. Lie here with only the whites of your eyes gleaming through the dark. To feel the bones sticking out of your skin. It will get me, too, like it got this guy. It is getting me. I can feel it. Twenty years before my time I will be like this guy. Maybe it will be in a mission like this, and they will come and carry me out on a stretcher. Maybe I will be lying in the corner of a box car with the roar of the wheels underneath me. Maybe it will come quick while I am shivering in a soup-line, a soup-line that stretches for a block and never starts moving. I lie up here on my three-decker bunk and shiver. I am not cold. I am afraid. What is a man to do? I know well enough what he can do. All he can do is to try to keep his belly full of enough slop so that he won't rattle when he breathes. All he can do is to

WAITING FOR NOTHING

try and find himself a lousy flop at night. Day after day, week after week, year after year, always the same—three hots and a flop.